About the editors

Kees Koonings is Associate Professor of Development Studies in the Faculty of Social Sciences, Utrecht University.

Dirk Kruijt is Professor of Development Studies in the Faculty of Social Sciences, Utrecht University.

They are the co-editors of three previously published Zed Books titles:

Societies of Fear: *The Legacy of Civil War, Violence and Terror in Latin America* (1999)

Political Armies: *The Military and Nation Building in the Age of Democracy* (2002)

Armed Actors: *Organised Violence and State Failure in Latin America* (2004)

KEES KOONINGS & DIRK KRUIJT | editors

Fractured cities

Social exclusion, urban violence and
contested spaces in Latin America

Zed Books
LONDON | NEW YORK

Fractured cities: Social exclusion, urban violence and contested spaces in Latin America was first published by Zed Books Ltd, 7 Cynthia Street, London N1 9JF, UK and Room 400, 175 Fifth Avenue, New York, NY 10010, USA in 2007.

www.zedbooks.co.uk

Cover designed by Andrew Corbett
Set in OurType Arnhem and Futura Bold by Ewan Smith, London
Index: <ed.emery@britishlibrary.net>
Printed and bound in Malta by Gutenberg Press Ltd

Distributed in the USA exclusively by Palgrave Macmillan, a division of St Martin's Press, LLC, 175 Fifth Avenue, New York, NY 10010.

A catalogue record for this book is available from the British Library.
US CIP data are available from the Library of Congress.

ISBN 1 84277 730 0 | 978 1 84277 730 5 hb
ISBN 1 84277 731 9 | 978 1 84277 731 2 pb

Contents

Tables and figures

Tables

Figures

Acknowledgements

The contributions to this book are inspired by a shared interest in and research experience of urban exclusion and violence in Latin America. The authors responded with enthusiasm to our initial call for chapters. With benign indulgence they agreed to work with a draft position paper that we circulated. Eventually this paper became the first chapter of the book. The subsequent chapters, the city case studies, each display a particular flavour that reflects both the authors' preferences and varying local conditions of exclusion and violence; the closing chapter explores the experiences of violence of the urban poor in general. We are grateful to the Department of Anthropology of Utrecht University, and especially Kootje Willemse, for supporting our work in compiling and editing this volume. Finally, we owe the usual debt to the team at Zed Books, in particular Ellen McKinlay, for guiding us through the final stages of editing and production.

Kees Koonings and Dirk Kruijt
Utrecht, February 2006

Introduction: the duality of Latin American cityscapes

KEES KOONINGS AND DIRK KRUIJT

The high expectations about Latin America's future nurtured by many a quarter of a century ago have largely vanished into thin air. This continent of largely urban societies is essentially fractured, showing a basic duality of rich and poor, formal and informal, organized and disintegrated, ruled and unruled, separated and linked at the same time. Around 1980, the approaching end of the historical cycle of inward-oriented development, authoritarian politics and – in a number of countries – open civil war was widely received as a promise of renewed economic dynamism, social welfare, democratic politics and citizenship. Two decades of neo-liberal reforms, formal democratization and globalizing urban modernity, however, have produced nothing but disillusion for the 50–70 per cent of urban denizens estimated to live on the wrong side of the breach of poverty, insecurity and exclusion. This echoes a wider set of problems emerging across the region: the persistently high social costs of the neo-liberal economic model, the performance and representation gap of formal democracy, the alarmingly low levels of social trust in general and trust in politics and public institutions in particular, and the proliferation of violence and fear leading to a pervasive sensation of insecurity among every sector of the population.

Nowhere does this seem more acute than in Latin America's cities. The traditional social cleavages appear to have become wider and more intense. Poverty has become an urban phenomenon in the region. The urban middle classes, once seen as the harbingers of modernity and social advancement, now live under siege. Local administrations are overwhelmed by the task of governing conflicting interests and providing basic public services. The growing perception of this urban crisis is therefore clearly not limited to the poor, who in most large conurbations have become the majority of urbanites. It affects the totality of urban social formations in Latin America. The fragmentation and deterioration of the urban space or 'cityscape' through inequality, insecurity and fear affect the lives of the elites and the middle class as much as they do the poor. Latin American cities in fact constitute a coexistence of contradictory social and spatial elements within the same social-geographical space.

1

In this context, the notion of urban insecurity, violence and fear have in recent years taken on the signal role earlier performed by notions such as poverty, marginality and informality. But violence and fear cannot, obviously, be assessed in isolation. It is necessary to study these phenomena not only in their broader sociological and anthropological context but also from the point of view of how they are lived and perceived. Both perspectives point at the multi-dimensionality of insecurity, violence and fear and at the multiple aspects of social reality tied up in their various manifestations. An often used starting point is the convergence of poverty and violence. Indeed, poverty can breed violence, the poor are disproportionally affected by violence, and the poor are often seen and feared as inherently violent and dangerous (mostly by the well-to-do, of course). Violence, through the notions of vulnerability and insecurity, has been incorporated into mainstream objective and subjective notions of poverty and social exclusion.

Yet we feel that it is worthwhile to make an attempt at a broader, comprehensive analysis of the current urban predicament in Latin America. The chapter brought together in this volume address, each in its own particular way, the interaction between inequality and exclusion, informalization, urban politics and public administration, the (un)rule of law, and the role of armed actors and violence brokers in the Latin American cityscape. Most chapters deal with these issues in case studies of particular cities. Below we will briefly highlight five key themes that run through the contributions; together they constitute the archetype of the present-day dual cityscape in Latin America.

The first issue and the starting point is the long-standing syndrome of urban poverty, inequality and social exclusion. Although this has been part and parcel of Latin American patterns of urbanization over the past century or so, the new neo-liberal model that dominated the past two decades has intensified this pattern to a considerable degree. In the first chapter, we elaborate on some of the aspects of urban poverty and exclusion, emphasizing in particular the process of informalization. This does not merely mean making a living in the so-called informal sector but envelops broader aspects of social life such as grassroots organizations, community-level sociability, political practices and identification. Here we should observe that the relationship between, on the one hand, poverty, exclusion and informality and, on the other hand, violence and fear is by no means direct or automatic. The majority of poor people simply try to make ends meet in as decent a way as possible. Poverty and exclusion, however, form the backdrop to violence and fear in the sense that they lower barriers and inhibitions and tend to make non-violent practices less attractive and legitimate. Not only do the well-to-do and local governments

2

often associate poor people with violence (as agents, an association heavily loaded with stigma), as is shown by Cathy McIlwaine and Caroline Moser in the final chapter of this volume, but the poor themselves also experience violence as victims, as the principal problem in everyday life. This aspect comes up in most of the case studies presented in the book.

A second issue addressed throughout the book is the withdrawal (if not failure) of the (local) state, especially of its public security functions. The widening of so-called governance voids and the unrule of law is now acknowledged as an important element in the relationship between urban exclusion, insecurity and violence. In many cases, the police and the judiciary are ineffective in dealing with crime and violence, or worse, are among the active protagonists. This failure is partial or selective, however, roughly following a class/colour divide; hence 'state abandonment' might be a more appropriate term. As is clearly demonstrated by Elizabeth Leeds for Rio de Janeiro (in Chapter 2), Wil Pansters and Hector Castillo Berthier for Mexico City (in Chapter 3) and Roberto Briceño-León for Caracas (in Chapter 6), local official security forces are often ineffective owing to disorganization, lack of vision, political disputes or an overly militarized approach to law enforcement and public security. In Rio de Janeiro and particularly in Medellín, the police have even been part of a veritable urban war. As a result, in many Latin American cities, the police are highly distrusted and often seen as a threat by inhabitants of low-income neighbourhoods. Lima, as argued by Dirk Kruijt and Carlos Iván Degregori in Chapter 7, seems to be a deviant case where the police have managed to preserve a civilian and pro-citizen orientation and reputation.

This specific form of state fragility has contributed, additionally, to the recent proliferation of armed actors and violence brokers in Latin American cities. The most spectacular case has been provided by Medellín. Ralph Rozema shows in Chapter 4 how, since the late 1980s, the cityscape of Colombia's second city has been occupied by a succession of armed actors who have all been linked to the wider armed conflict at the national level: the original drugs cartels and their *sicarios* (assassins), criminal gangs, leftist militias and guerrilla forces, right-wing paramilitary and mafia control outfits (*oficinas*), as well as the army and the police. But in many other cities the usual violence brokers are the youth gangs. Against the backdrop of exclusion and the lack of educational, economic and social options faced primarily by male youngsters, urban gangs have emerged as alternative vehicles for social order, integration and power. Moser and McIlwaine (2004 and ch. 8, this volume) call these 'perverse organizations'. Leeds (1996 and ch. 2, this volume) uses the notion of 'parallel powers', which have been growing in strength in Rio

3

de Janeiro's *favelas* and even in the city as a whole. The cases of Rio, Medellín and also Managua clearly show the various mechanisms of recruitment, dominance and even a certain acceptance of the gangs, according them legitimacy. The youngsters look for economic opportunities, alternative ways of social integration and belonging, personal and community status, personal and neighbourhood protection, power, and even cultural distinction in newly shaped social hierarchies. In Chapter 5, Dennis Rodgers vividly shows how in the Managua *barrio* he studied the local drugs gang has been the linchpin for the accumulation of wealth and status in which conspicuous consumption takes on a notable role. Another ominous form of violence brokerage is extralegal or even mob justice. Lynchings dealing with (suspected) petty criminals or other unfamiliar outsiders are an increasingly disturbing phenomenon in Latin American cities (as exemplified for Mexico City by Pansters and Castillo in Chapter 3).

Further, the syndrome of insecurity, violence and fear has given rise to a new brand of survival 'know-how': coping with insecurity and violence in everyday life. McIlwaine and Moser argue in Chapter 8 that the residents of poor areas in the Colombian and Guatemalan cities and towns they studied face a series of restrictions in how they use time, space and social relations. Similar observations are made for Caracas by Briceño-León (in Chapter 6) and for Medellín by Rozema (in Chapter 4). Again, Lima seems to be an exception; Degregori and Kruijt describe, in Chapter 7, the relative safety of the micro-business, shopping and leisure areas in this city's poor districts.

Finally, the thematic explorations and especially the city studies brought together in this volume strongly suggest a new urban duality as both cause and consequence, in a classic Hegelian dialectic, or more prosaically a vicious circle, of exclusion, insecurity and violence. It is not just livelihood strategies which have become informalized, but also social organization, social order, social status and social identities. This has caused a social and spatial fragmentation of Latin American cities. Poverty and violence are often associated with certain neighbourhoods or districts that become stigmatized as no-go areas while their inhabitants are in turn stigmatized as 'undesirables'. This has structural and enduring consequences for the lives of the majorities in Latin American urban agglomerations. They are ignored by those social sectors that do take part in urban consumerism and modernity, and are targeted by the security forces as the new social enemies. At best, a class of second-rate or informal citizens is constituted, for whom insecurity has become a permanent fact of life.

Is there an antidote? The contributions in this book do not offer alternatives or prescriptions since the purpose has been analytical rather than policy-oriented. A few tentative ingredients of an alternative model may, however, be mentioned. Some of these elements appear to have been relevant in Lima, presented here as an exceptional (although of course not problem-free) case, especially considering the magnitude of poverty in Peru's capital and the recent history of mass rural–urban migration and political violence. A first and obvious ingredient seems to be a constructive public presence, especially on the part of local, decentralized administrations, that makes the provision of basic public services (including law enforcement) its key priority. Second, an approach to public security and law enforcement should be based on the notion of citizenship rights. Here, sensibility to the specific constraints faced by poor citizens should prevail over futile zero-tolerance or militarized approaches (the latter often driven by political pressure from middle-class constituencies). Sustainable police reform, isolated from political whims and quarrels, is a necessary but not sufficient element. Finally, opening spaces for community participation, in local governance in general and in security issues in particular, may help in restoring the effectiveness and above all the legitimacy of dealing with the urban predicament in a civic way.

1 | Fractured cities, second-class citizenship and urban violence

KEES KOONINGS AND DIRK KRUIJT

Against the background of painful economic adjustment, persistent social inequality and uncertain democratic consolidation, the problem of urban violence in Latin America has been the subject of a growing number of empirical studies and conceptual debates in recent years. These scholarly activities in turn link up with growing public and political concern about poverty, inequality and violence in a region in which almost 75 per cent of the population live in cities.

The long-term background to these phenomena is the rapid demographic expansion of Latin American cities, especially during the second half of the last century, in combination with the limited absorption capacity of the urban labour markets and the inability of local governments to provide basic public services. This has led to the growth of urban poverty, initially seen in terms of 'marginality', implying its atypical and temporary nature. From the 1970s onwards, poverty and inequality were recognized as persistent phenomena and came to be studied as part of broader structures of socio-economic heterogeneity, but also from the perspective of social exclusion and survival strategies beyond the realm of formal markets and institutions (Perlman 1976). Since the 1980s, informality has been one of the key terms with which to designate the complex configuration of livelihood, social relations and identity construction in the poor parts of Latin American cities. Especially in the so-called megacities (but also in smaller national capitals and secondary cities), informality and social exclusion defined an urban society that was increasingly separated, spatially, socially and culturally, from the (lower and upper) middle-class city of formal employment, public services and law enforcement (Portes 1989).

These patterns of exclusion have deepened over the past two decades. Across Latin America urban poverty is persistent; urban crime and violence are on the rise; the effective presence of state authorities is minimal and the rule of law has changed into its antithesis. Within this context, urban denizens face violence and fear. The absence or failure of governance (especially the enforcement and protection of citizens' security) opens the way for a variety of armed actors and violence brokers who carve out alternative, informal spheres of power on the basis of coercion. The result is in many cases a fragmented,

7

ambivalent and hybrid cityscape with varying manifestations of the complex of poverty, exclusion, coercion, violence and fear.

In this chapter, we will discuss the principal issues at stake. First we will review the development of urban poverty, informality and social exclusion in Latin America during the past decades. Then we will briefly enter the conceptual debate on social exclusion, (in)security and the so-called 'new violence'. Subsequently we will trace the outlines and types of contemporary urban violence, the armed actors involved and the consequences in terms of the failure of the rule of law and governance. We will then note the concomitant rise of parallel power structures (Leeds 1996) that can be regarded as informal modes of control and coercion in Latin American cities. We will address the question of how these patterns of coercion and violence affect community organizations, civil society and politics, both at the grass roots and at broader levels of society.

Urban poverty, *desborde popular* and the erosion of the formal social order

Second-class citizenship in Latin America has been associated, traditionally, with the indigenous populations, the underdeveloped rural hinterland and the fragmented land tenure of the *comunidades indígenas*. In colonial times, the *encomienda*, the *mita* and the *hacienda* system had tied the Mexican, Central American and Andean conquered ethnicities to their *criollo* landlord and *peninsular* governors. With good reason, De la Peña (1980) typified the post-colonial descendants, the indigenous and rural underprivileged, as 'heirs of promises': promises of integration in the national community, promises of citizenship without citizens' rights and duties (Bastos 1998: 100–101). For that reason Solares (1992: 50) typified Guatemala as 'a state without being a nation'. And for the same reason Flores Galindo (1994: 213) characterized Peru, with its political coexistence of *mestizos* and *indios*, as 'a republic without citizens'.[1]

In the second half of the twentieth century, however, the pattern of segregation, restriction, poverty and de facto second-class citizenship acquired an urban face. In another publication, on the dynamics of urban poverty, informality and social exclusion in Latin America (Kruijt, Sojo and Grynszpan 2002), we introduced the notion of 'informal citizenship', the precarious implantation of (urban) second-class citizenship, as the long-term result of the mainstream model of economic reforms in the 1980s and 1990s. This instability is related to a trans-generational process of informalization and social exclusion in the urban, and more precisely the metropolitan, environments, nourished by a continuous migration stream from the rural hinterland

8

TABLE 1.1 Evolution of urban poverty and inequality in Latin America and selected countries (1990–2002)

	1990	1997	2002
Total poverty (headcount)	48.3	43.5	44.0
Urban poverty (headcount)	41.4	36.5	38.4
Urban extreme poverty (headcount)	15.3	12.3	13.5
Urban income distribution in selected countries (Gini index):			
Argentina	0.501	0.530	0.590
Brazil	0.606	0.620	0.628
Colombia	–	0.577	0.575
Guatemala	0.558	0.525	0.524
Mexico	0.530	0.507	0.477
Peru	–	0.473	0.477

Source: Authors' elaboration of poverty indices based on survey data from nineteen countries (drawn from CEPAL 2004).

which started in the 1950s and 1960s in most of the countries of Latin America and the larger island states of the Caribbean. Between 1950 and 1980, the share of Latin America's informal economy grew steadily, only to accelerate in the 1980s and 1990 (Galli and Kucera 2003: 24–6). Latin America has thus become the continent in which in most of its countries a significant segment of the population is, at once, poor, informal and excluded.

Using UNDP, ECLAC and ILO data over the last twenty years, we can discern a number of trends. In the first place, poverty, informality and social exclusion have become a massive urban phenomenon. Aggregate statistical data from 1990 to the early 2000s show a consistent proportion of the urban income poor in Latin America of more than one-third of the total urban population, with a tendency to increase after 2000 (see Table 1.1). With the urban population still growing (and at a significantly faster rate than the rural population) during the 1990s, the absolute number of urban poor increased. In 2002, roughly 144 million (or 65 per cent) out of the total 221 million of income poor in Latin America lived in cities and towns. Fifty million people lived in extreme poverty (*indigencia*).[2] This development is reflected in persistent and often increasing inequality in the distribution of urban income and wealth and in the geographic layout of Latin America's metropolis, in which the expansion of slums and the deterioration of popular neighbourhoods have become clearly visible over the past two or three decades.

In the second place, urban poverty has become increasingly heterogeneous, reflecting marked changes within the Latin American urban class structures (Portes 1985; Portes and Hoffman 2003). The chronically poor are now joined by the 'new poor', descending from the strata of the middle and industrial working classes. Old and new poor converge in the bulging sector of informal micro-entrepreneurs and self-employed in search of survival and livelihood strategies. The decomposition of the urban working class has led not only to the formation of a new urban social stratification but also to changes in the size and composition of poor households' family structures. The traditional role of men as heads of families is ebbing away with the growing number of female-headed households in the working-class neighbourhoods. Furthermore, the informal economy and society even generates hidden migration cycles, demographic breakdowns and cleavages within the family structure.

Central America, with its poverty-stricken and war-torn societies, perhaps provides the best example of disruption at the family level. Mahler (2002) presents an overview of the Central American intra- and extra-regional migration processes: the displacement process of war refugees fleeing violence and the extra-regional migration, in fact a population exodus, to Mexico and the USA. Their remittances keep the informal societies of El Salvador, Guatemala, Honduras and Nicaragua afloat. Data from Pérez Saínz (2004) substantiate this pattern of dependency on remittances, a structurally reduced employment market, unemployment among women and younger people, broken families and the despair of the family at home after the 'temporary' migration of the male members, and the bitter choice between self-employment and emigration.

Meanwhile, the social categories that have always been associated with poverty and exclusion (ethnic sectors and indigenous peoples) have retained and consolidated that traditional profile. Ethnicity is a stratifying factor within the urban informal economy and society. Mechanisms for survival predominate: ties of ethnicity, religion, real or symbolic family relationships, closeness to the place of birth, local neighbourhood relations. The informal economy has more to do with black people than the black market. In the Andean countries, in Central America and Mexico, features of Quechua or Mayan culture mix with elements of informal society.

This river of poverty and exclusion bursting its banks and generating this new basin of informality and second-class citizenship was portrayed, in the early 1980s, by Peruvian anthropologist Matos Mar (1984) as the *desborde popular*. In a prophetic essay he depicted the decline of the institutional pillars of traditional Peruvian society, overwhelmed by the mushrooming of

Lima's *pueblos jovenes* (new villages) – the political euphemism for a massive popular invasion of poor-quality urban terrain – and its consequences in terms of the emergence of a qualitatively new urban society. He also predicted the timid birth of a diversity of organizations representing the informal entrepreneurs and self-employed, such as local and regional chambers of craftsmen and *comedores populares* (community-run canteens offering cheap meals in the slums of Lima Metropolitana). What all these have in common is an ambivalent relationship of dependency on professional development organizations, such as religious and ecclesiastical foundations, NGOs, donor agencies, private banks 'with a social face', and municipal and central government organizations, their financiers.

In an updated version of his essay, published twenty years later (Matos Mar 2004), he took into account the collapse of the traditional support institutions of the democratic order: the decline of political parties, the erosion of the status of the legislature and the judiciary, the dwindling stature of magistrates as the legitimate authorities in the sphere of law and order, the collapse of the once powerful trade union confederations, and the weakening of other conventional entities of civil society, such as the chambers of industry and commerce, the professional organizations of doctors, lawyers and engineers, etc. Twenty-first-century Peru, and Latin America as a whole, is, in his opinion, 'a national society that is incomplete and unfinished, not authentic, a half-way formed Republic, to be reconstructed, revaluated and revitalised to create the possibility of [...] full, participatory citizenship with (national) identity' (ibid.: 116).

Matos Mar none the less ends on a note of optimism, as if informality and exclusion were syndromes to be overcome in time, particularly through deliberate social and political reform. But is such an agenda of reinstitution-alization feasible? The parallel institutions, hierarchies and sectors that have emerged in the wake of poverty, informality and social exclusion may well have formed a more durable, albeit heterogeneous, economic, social, political and cultural order. Formal and informal institutions regulate themselves with their own types of logic, morality and sanctions: the civil order of the formal economy and society, and the semi-anarchy of poverty, informality and social exclusion.

From *desborde popular* to *desborde de la violencia*: conceptualizing exclusion, insecurity and violence

Urban second-class citizenship is also citizenship with a violent face. At the end of the 1970s, Walton (1976, 1977) introduced the concept of 'divided cities'. In the 1970s and 1980s, the 'divided' or 'fragmented' cities were mostly typified in terms of urban misery or social exclusion and were described in terms of the dichotomy between elites and well-to-do middle classes versus the 'forgotten' slum dwellers. The intertwined dynamics of social exclusion and proliferation of violence had also acquired clear spatial dimensions. This has been noted by numerous authors (e.g. Portes 1989; Caldeira 2000; Rolnik 1999). Urban segregation refers not only to the geographical distribution of the traditional markers of poverty (human deprivation, dilapidated housing, absent services and degraded public spaces) but also to the territorial and social division of cities in 'go' and 'no-go' areas, at least from the perspective of the middle-class citizen and local public administration. The shanty towns came to be seen as veritable enclaves that obeyed a totally different set of rules and codes of conduct.

From the 1990s on, however, the concept of the urban divide began to be identified with the 'unrule of law' (Méndez et al. 1999), the lack of human security and the absence of security and law-enforcing authorities in the neglected parts of the urban territory. The case of Rio de Janeiro, whose poverty-stricken and crime-ridden *favelas* are synonymous with 'no-go areas' within the metropolitan boundaries, acquired a depressing reputation among researchers and authors dealing with urban violence. Ventura's (2002 [1994]) publication on the *cidade partida* was to be followed by other publications.[3] After restudying the *favelas* and their inhabitants featured in her late 1960s and early 1970s research thirty years later, Perlman (2005: 22) arrives at the sobering conclusion that the 'myth of marginality' has changed into the 'reality of marginality'. Her new study shows that urban violence and insecurity, linked to the stigma of living in a *favela*, are the most powerful mechanisms contributing to the 'new marginality'. The relationship between the recent increase of poverty and violence in Buenos Aires was discussed, in comparative terms, by Saín (2002). Pécaut (2001, 2003) discussed extensively the Colombian situation, where urban social exclusion, crime and violence became part of the vortex of large-scale drugs-based organized crime and political violence within the country's 'degenerated' civil conflict (PNUD 2003).

In other words, the connection between urban poverty, insecurity and violence has been reformulated in terms of the 'violent' failure of citizenship. Here it might be useful to bring in the concept of 'citizen security'. Although we run the risk here of adding to the already growing terminological confusion with respect to poverty, exclusion, vulnerability and insecurity, the notion of citizen security can be used to establish a conceptual link between poverty, exclusion, state failure and violence. The term echoes the notion of human security that has served to bring concern for poverty and vulnerability, in short human welfare and those factors that put it at risk, into the study of conflict, violence and security (UNDP 1994; World Bank 2000). It is true that this effort to direct the security notion away from an exclusive focus on the (military) threats of (territorial) states to the threats of individuals and communities has to a certain degree overstretched the security concept (Paris 2001).[4] We suggest here that human security should mean the freedom of individuals and communities from threats posed by conflict and violence to their physical, social or cultural integrity or survival. Citizen security further narrows this notion down by saying that freedom from violence should be seen as part of the citizenship status of individuals and communities. That is to say, individuals and communities are, ideally, citizens because they are rights-bearers to the extent that they are incorporated into nation-states and (increasingly but tentatively) into an international community which abide by the principles of democracy, rule of law and humanitarian standards. Therefore, human security should be guaranteed in the public domain within a framework of citizenship rights.

Poverty in itself will not normally generate systematic or organized violence. But persistent social exclusion, linked to alternative extra-legal sources of income and power, combined with an absent or failing state in particular territorial/social settings, will provide means and motives for violent actions, which contribute in turn to a disintegration of the social and moral fabric. Urban violence in Latin America can thus be seen as a typical manifestation of citizenship insecurity, because citizenship, democratic governance and the rule of law are at the same time embraced by intellectuals, NGOs and political elites as guiding principles for contemporary social development in the region and ignored or regarded as inconsequentual by a significant proportion of the region's (urban) population (Koonings and Kruijt 2004). Citizenship insecurity not only has this element of (partial) state failure and the fragmentation of rights, but is also reflected in the practices and perceptions of those living in the contemporary urban no-go areas: the restriction of the freedom to move and to act socially, the feeling of discrimination and stigmatization, the imminence of danger in the face of abandonment or even victimization by the forces of law and order and 'extra-legal' armed actors alike.

The social and cultural dimensions of contemporary urban violence and fear in Latin America's metropolitan territories were comparatively analysed and illustrated for the first time in a collection of articles and essays edited by Rotker (2002). Moser and McIlwaine (2004) published the results of a

Fractured cities

systematic and comparative study on urban violence as perceived by the urban poor. They distinguish between social, economic and political categories of violence. Social violence covers domestic violence, both inside and outside the home, including child abuse. Economic violence includes street crime (mugging, robbing, drugs-related violence and kidnapping) and is motivated by material gain. Political violence encompasses guerrilla and paramilitary conflict, internal wars and political assassination. It is interesting to observe how consistently the urban poor in nationwide surveys and group interviews comment on the complex interconnections between the different sources of violence.

Violence, however, is not only firmly rooted in the daily lives of the metropolitan and urban poor but is also a characteristic of the long-lasting civil wars in Central America and the Andean countries. In two previous publications (Kruijt and Koonings 1999; Koonings and Kruijt 2004) we analysed the shift from state-induced violence, the legacy of state terror of the Latin American military dictatorships in the 1960s, 1970s and 1980s, to the violence stemming from non-state actors operating in urban 'violence enclaves' and disputing urban territories, generally the habitat of the urban poor. Armed actors with a military background, criminal gangs, youth bands and ordinary criminal gangs have managed to institute parallel systems of violence of national significance in countries such as Colombia, Guatemala and Mexico, and, to a lesser degree or on a more localized scale, in Argentina, Brazil and Peru. Colombia and Guatemala are, sadly, two good examples of causality chains between nationwide violence and local violence enclaves. Post-war Guatemala is infested by new forms of violence caused by street gangs, former paramilitary forces and former military and police personnel involved in drugs trafficking. In Colombia the *desborde de la violencia* has become institutionalized during the last couple of decades. Political conflict in Colombia has also been intensified by drug-linked violence and local criminality. The civil war in this country is reproduced at local level by micro-wars in the metropolitan areas and the urban *comunas*.

Armed actors and violence brokers

It is interesting to note that, in the context of permeating violence and fluctuating mini-wars about small territories, the Latin American armed forces usually do not play a substantial role. During the long years of military dictatorship, civil-military governments and civil wars the armed forces were the principal actors in state-related violence, directed against the internal enemies of the state: revolutionary movements, guerrilla forces, peasant *frentes*, union leaders and presumed 'communists'. State terror and the complicated apparatus of repression, formed by the system of interlinked intelligence services, state security forces, paramilitary units and ancillary police, created 'societies of fear' at the national level, intensified in combat zones and theatres of counter-insurgency against guerrilla forces and other insurgents. In the 1990s, during the process of withdrawal of the military governments and the transition to civilian governments, the military presence that had manifested itself in the past was transformed into a shadow presence, through the 'compulsory military advisers' and 'civil–military ties' between the public sector, the intelligence service and the leading generals. While even in the twenty-first century the (military) intelligence services and state security bureaucracies in many Andean and Central American countries are still focused on activities against the internal enemies of the state, the armed forces in the southern cone countries have publicly withdrawn from the political arena, reformulating their objectives clearly as those of 'professional soldiers' (Koonings and Kruijt 2002; Kruijt and Koonings 2004). The armed forces are leaving the direct confrontation with non-state violent actors to the police and the special police forces, more adapted to urban aggression and explicitly trained in counter-aggression. In the early 1990s, efforts to deploy the Brazilian armed forces to restore law and order in the *favelas* of Rio de Janeiro met with failure. In Medellín, the relative success of the army's Operation Orion, in which the security forces intervened in 2002 in the ongoing politico-criminal urban war, merely paved the way for the strengthening of the position of the paramilitary forces of the Cacique Nutibara and Metro groups in the poor *comunas*.

What we do observe is the proliferation of 'private vigilantism': private police, privately paid street guardians in the middle-class and even the working-class metropolitan districts, private citizens' *serenazgos* (nightwatch committees or private protection squads), special forces in the financial sector recruited from former police forces and the army, extra-legal task forces, paramilitary commandos, death squads, and so on. These were a legacy of the prolonged civil wars in countries such as Colombia and Guatemala, but gradually extended to the urban spaces in the majority of the Latin American countries and some Caribbean island states, such as Jamaica, confronted with this 'new violence'. At the same time, continuous fragmentation of the military and paramilitary organizations and in some cases the guerrilla forces of the civil wars in Colombia, Guatemala and Peru contributed to a more hidden, more ambiguous scenario of semi-organized crime and extortion of public functionaries and private persons.

Then there are the new urban warlords of local violence: the chiefs among the *barrio*'s drugs traffickers, the leaders of the *maras* (criminal youth gangs) in the slums of Central America, the monopoly holders of local illegal violence, however accepted. They are the new enforcers of customary justice, harsh but clear. They are the new local tax collectors who distribute the revenues. Anomalies such as the regular funding, by drugs money, of local NGOs operating in the slums of Rio de Janeiro, Gran Buenos Aires and the three major Colombian cities of Bogotá, Medellín and Cali are common. The *traficantes* wish to express their benevolence towards local development. For instance, Deusimar da Costa, president of the Federaçao Municipal das Asociações de Favelas do Rio de Janeiro (FEMAFARJ/FAR-Rio), acknowledged quite frankly that peaceful coexistence with the *traficantes* was a fact of life. 'They are *moradores* [residents],' she said, 'and their presence does not trouble us. They have the power of intervention and they are *moradores*, after all. We share, as you would call it, a symbiotic life. We are not inclined to call in the police.'[5] The local drugs gangs can also express their territorial aspirations by, for instance, closing, temporarily at least, the highway to the airport, as happened several times in Rio de Janeiro on the instructions of different *favela* chiefs. In some cases, they explicitly negotiate spheres of influence with the local church leaders. Jonas Pedreina, president of the association of *moradores* in one of the *favelas* in northern Rio de Janeiro and an evangelical church leader, declared that the local drugs boss had offered to finance all church, NGO and *asociação* activities, 'no strings attached'. The pastor and the *favela* leader had refused his offer.[6] In daily practice the drug economy and the churches have learned to respect each other and to maintain relations of peaceful coexistence.

The necessities of daily coexistence cannot hide the fact that drugs bosses and gang leaders in Argentina's *villas*, Brazil's *favelas*, Colombia's *tugurios* and Central American *barrios* have transposed national war scenarios on to urban territorial disputes. Several thousand child and adolescent soldiers in Rio de Janeiro operate in drug gang wars. The relationship between youth gangs and drugs trafficking was typified by Zaluar (2000, 2001, 2004) as 'perverse integration' in the clandestine economy. A similar pattern is offered by the Colombian *sicarios* that have made violence into a strategy not only for income generation but also for status and prestige in the neighbourhood (Salazar 1993a, 1993b).

The involvement of youth is not a specific South American phenomenon: in the Central American countries of El Salvador, Honduras, Guatemala and to a lesser extent Nicaragua, the *maras* are national security threat number one (Rodgers 1999; Savenije and Van der Borgh 2004; Savenije and Andrade-Eekhoff 2003). Tens of thousands of children and young adults, aged between twelve and thirty years, belong to one of the *maras* or *pandillas juveniles*, which in El Salvador and Honduras accounted for 45 per cent and in Guatemala for 20 per cent of the homicides in 2003 (Peetz 2004).[7] The Central American *marero* economy depends on territorial control and drugs trafficking. The scale of youth gang operations is so extended that recently special anti-*mara* legislation was approved by parliament and security commandos were formed by police forces and military personnel in Honduras (Operación Libertad, 2003) and El Salvador (Plan Mano Dura, 2003). The number of victims of *mara* incidents has already surpassed the number of victims of the civil war in El Salvador. This brings us to the broader political and social implications of Latin America's urban violence, which we will discuss in the following sections.

The politics of urban violence

The many different mini-war scenarios in Latin America and the Caribbean and the proliferation of the (urban) armed actors involved are related to the phenomenon of local 'governance voids'. Pinheiro (1996) and Méndez et al. (1999) have argued convincingly that one of the key aspects of contemporary urban poverty and social exclusion is the failure of the state to guarantee citizens' security and the rule of law vis-à-vis what they euphemistically call the 'underprivileged'. This failure is reflected in the incapacity to protect citizens from everyday and organized violence, but also in the involvement of state agencies – or members of these agencies – in arbitrary, extra-legal and criminal violence. In recent research, the role of the police (and ancillary policing; see Van Reenen 2004) particularly has been brought to the fore.

Governance voids exist where the legal authorities and the representatives of law and order are absent and, consequently, a local vacuum of 'regular' law and order is created (Kruijt and Koonings 1999: 12). In this vacuum a kind of osmotic symbiosis emerges between the state (the police, the law system) and 'common' criminality and criminalized former members of the armed forces, the police, paramilitary units and guerrilla combatants. 'Law and order' is then the result of a fluctuating order of parallel forces of local power players and 'moral' authorities (elected representatives of associations of *vecinos*, *pobladores* or *moradores*, priests and evangelical pastors, even successful entrepreneurs or owners of radio and TV stations) in shifting alliances. The political dimension of this phenomenon is that the local state and its agents oscillate between selective involvement, insulation and outright abandonment. In these voids, alternative, informal or 'parallel' structures arise, seeking various forms of confrontation or accommodation with the legitimate authorities and with civil society.

Three elements come together. First, there is the paradox of rising crime under conditions of political democratization and post-conflict peace building. As a general rule this leads to pressure from key electoral constituencies for tough crime-fighting policies. In many cases this is picked up by neo-populist or delegative democracy politicians who endorse hardline approaches. Second, the forces of the law themselves often operate with a militarized logic of law enforcement on the basis of the repression rather than the observance of rights. This is a legacy of authoritarianism and national security doctrines, but the 'enemy' now is the 'marginal, criminal element' rather than the leftist political opponent. This logic in fact puts law enforcement above the law, since the agents of the public security forces make the law by applying it. This goes *a fortiori* for the privatized functions of law enforcement, whether through security companies or (even) more murky forms of vigilantism. In practice, public and private law enforcement merges because of the involvement of serving, dismissed or retired police officers in private security endeavours and death squads. A key problem here is the widespread impunity enjoyed by public and private 'violence workers' (Huggins et al. 2002). Third, this violence builds upon a long-standing internal culture of hierarchy, privilege and abuse within the security forces themselves, which helps to erode the adherence to principles of legality, rights and due process that should be expected from democratic security forces (Glebbeek 2003).

This means that the 'democratically' generated demand for tough security measures produces blatant anti-democratic practices of arbitrariness and violence that are not kept in check by democratic forces within political or civil society and are very seldom addressed through the legal system. Instead it leads to the routine practice of the *gatillo facil* (easy trigger), as it is dubbed in Argentina, which clearly negates the principle of citizenship. In fact, arbitrary, extra-legal violence by security forces reproduces and deepens existing patterns of inequality and social exclusion since the victims (whether criminals or innocent) are to be found predominantly among the excluded social sectors, second- and third-class citizens on the basis of class, ethnicity and age for whom the principles of democracy and rule of law do not apply in practice (Pinheiro 1996; Méndez et al. 1999). In other words, law enforcement often equals social cleansing. Furthermore, this state of affairs creates conditions for the symbiosis of security forces and local criminal organizations, to be discussed below.

It may be clear that in such situations other public agencies not responsible for law enforcement but rather for the provision of other public goods and services find it hard if not impossible to function and keep their footing. As a consequence, for many poor urban denizens a violent police is the only face of the state that they see.

Parallel power and perverse integration

The constraints of social exclusion, the stigma of second-class or informal citizenship and the voids left by state incapacity in many areas contribute to the emergence of alternative forms of social organization. Access to the means of violence (facilitated by the material and social legacy of internal conflicts, drugs money and the proliferation of small arms; see Renner 1997) has made violence and coercion the prime foundation of such forms. Power, in terms of territorial and social control, extractive capabilities and de facto political prerogatives, is organized on the basis of access to de-officialized, decentralized and fractured means of violence. Status and legitimacy within local urban spaces are derived from the position one occupies within the system of coercion.

Elizabeth Leeds (1996) developed the notion of parallel power to analyse the control wielded by drugs gangs (and their *donos*, lords) within the poor neighbourhoods. This power depends not only on the gangs' capacity to impose 'law and order' on the local population, but also on their ability to infiltrate or control grassroots movements and to negotiate with (or impose conditions upon) the functioning of government and non-governmental agencies. Alba Zaluar (e.g. 2004) coined the notion of 'perverse integration' for the role of criminal gangs and forms of violent behaviour as alternative routes to status, acceptance and prestige, especially for young males. Similar mechanisms are at play in the case of the Central American *maras*.

The consequences of these alternative modes of integration and control for political power are not likely to be restricted to the grassroots level of the *favela* or the *barrio*. Often quite literally, the lords of the no-go areas 'go' into the world of respectability to exert pressure and to confirm their aspirations as power brokers. In some cases this *desborde* of parallel power has acquired national significance. The coercive strategy of organized crime showed itself openly in Colombia during the late 1980s and early 1990s. Led by Pablo Escobar, the drugs lords of the Medellín cartel unleashed rampant violence against public officials and public places to avert the prospect of extradition. More secretive strategies, such as those employed by the Cali cartel and the Mexican *traficantes*, relied on bribery and targeted violence to divert anti-drugs law enforcement operations and to gain a more pervasive influence within the corridors of political and state power. In Colombia this came to the fore during the Samper administration (1994–98), which greatly contributed to the defamation of democratic politics despite the high hopes induced by the 1991 constitutional reform (Thoumi 2002: 252–6).

As mentioned above, at the local level Brazil offers numerous examples of the way drugs gangs in cities like Rio de Janeiro and São Paulo employ explicit political strategies to consolidate their position in the *favelas* and to occupy or control local power spaces (Leeds 1996). The typical ingredients of this strategy are: the imposition of order and the administration of justice in the neighbourhood on the basis of the use of arbitrary force; the particularistic distribution of collective goods (a field in which the Colombian drug lord Pablo Escobar excelled); the infiltration or open takeover of local neighbourhood and dwellers' associations; and the corruption of police officers, civil servants and local politicians (Pandolfi and Grynszpan 2003). In this context, *quadrilha* (drugs gang) leaders and drugs barons have gained notoriety as alternative public figures.

Recently, drugs barons and urban gangs in general have made inroads into formal politics through open coercion. During the 2002 electoral campaign in Brazil, criminal gangs in Rio de Janeiro forced the closure of commercial premises and threatened to use violence against polling stations in order to generate a climate of fear. Apparently, the underlying objective was to send a message that the authorities (and the general public) should not try to encroach upon the de facto autonomous power spaces in the urban peripheries that are crucial for their control of the local drugs economy.

In Central America, the urban gangs known as *maras* or *pandillas* made a violent political debut in late 2003 in response to increasing government efforts to repress the gangs. In Honduras, the Maduro administration installed in 2001 had already been tightening the screws on *mara* activity. Some *maristas* had started negotiations with the government to discuss the terms of their disbanding and reintegration into mainstream social life. In October and November 2003, however, presumed M18 gang members brutally murdered a number of young women in San Pedro Sula, leaving indications (through notes and graffiti) that the *maras* refused to continue to conduct a dialogue with the authorities. Meanwhile, the presidents of Guatemala, Nicaragua, El Salvador and Honduras signed a covenant to step up concerted efforts to combat criminal urban gang violence.[8] In April 2005, the three chiefs of staff of the armed forces of El Salvador, Honduras and Guatemala asked the chief of the US Southern Command, General Bantz Craddock, for technical and financial assistance for their effort to ' ... create a joint Army and Police Special Force to combat drug trafficking and *mara* youth gangs'.[9] These developments echo the confrontations between the government, its US-assisted special forces and the Colombian drugs cartels more than a decade earlier.

Our deliberations pose questions about the stability of the political order based on widely generalized second-class citizenship. Informal citizenship in a context of violence seems to be the standard integration mechanism of the poor and the underprivileged. Considerable segments of the Latin American population survive in the informal economy and society, where poverty goes hand in hand with everyday violence. Many of the armed actors and power players are recruited from among the informals and the excluded. This phenomenon of social exclusion-cum-violence shared by the masses of the urban poor tends to destroy the foundations of the democratic order and its domains of citizenship. Continuous violence, even in restricted territorial enclaves, contributes to the erosion of legitimate governance. The paradox is that most Latin American governments, like many local popular leaders and church authorities before them, have accepted a de facto peaceful coexistence with the violent non-state actors, as long as they do not constitute a challenge to the national political order. The question is, of course, how long the economic, social and political order in Latin America can be maintained by this uneasy equilibrium between 'acceptable' levels of exclusion and 'acceptable' levels of violence.

Notes

1 This colonial and post-colonial exclusion pattern had consequences for early urban segregation. The colonial *vecinos* of the proud cities of Arequipa and Cartagena, descendants of the conquerors, denied *indios* access to the city. In other colonial cities and capitals special neighbourhoods were built to house the black population (in Lima, for instance) or the indigenous artisans (in Guadalajara; see Van Young 1981).

2 Calculated on the basis of data reported in CEPAL (2004: 2–4).

3 See, for instance, Barcellos 2003; Chaves Pandolfi and Grynszpan 2003; Evangelista 2003; Zaluar 1994, 2001.

4 Yet Paris's own solution to this problem only adds new variety to this confusion since he sees human security as military and/or non-military threats to societies, groups and individuals, with non-military threats apparently dominating the concept (2001: 98).

5 Interview, 28 August 2003, conducted by Dirk Kruijt.

6 Interview, 29 and 30 August 2003, conducted by Dirk Kruijt.

7 According to several sources, mentioned by Peetz (2004: 59), the number of

mareros varies between 14,000 and 20,000 in Guatemala, 10,500 and 35,000 in El Salvador, and 36,000 and 100,000 in Honduras. Nicaragua has perhaps 4,500 *mareros*, Costa Rica 2,600, Panama 1,385 and Belize 100.

8 See a notification entitled *Maduro, Berger, Flores y Bolaños contra las maras*, posted 14 January 2004 on the website of the Honduran presidential office, <www.casapresidencial.hn/2004/01/14_3.php>, consulted 24 March 2005.

9 *Siglo Veintiuno* (Guatemala), 15 April 2005.

2 | Rio de Janeiro

ELIZABETH LEEDS

Recent discussions of the 'new poverty' in Latin America, as distinct from the 'marginality' of the 1960s, point to such well-known macro causal factors as 1) the restructuring of the state resulting in government downsizing and privatization of essential services and 2) unequal globalization of trade and commerce leading to closure of industry, loss of jobs and growth of unemployment. Many argue that levels of exclusion and poverty are even greater today than in the decade of the 1960s and that symptoms of the new poverty – escalating rates of crime and violence – are qualitatively different from the poverty indicators of four decades ago.[1]

What else has changed in this almost half-century which might contribute to this deepening of exclusion? First, escalating rates of urbanization have reversed the urban/rural ratio of forty years ago. Brazil, for example, has a current urban/rural ratio of 70:30, the reverse of its demographic spread of the 1960s. Second, the process of industrialization of Brazil's largest cities from the 1940s to the 1960s – the phenomenon that stimulated the reversal of rural/urban ratios – has itself changed qualitatively. The kind of industry that employed many *favela* residents in the 1960s and 1970s has decreased markedly, either moving elsewhere within Brazil or to cheaper labour markets elsewhere in the world. Figures for the Rio Metropolitan Area for the decade of the 1990s show a 14 per cent decrease in jobs in the formal sector and a 30 per cent and 15 per cent increase in, respectively, 'autonomous' and 'informal' workers (Souza e Silva and Urani 2002). Third, and related to the first two, crime rates and levels of violence, especially in urban areas, have risen vertiginously in Latin America in this period.[2] The sense of insecurity from growing levels of violence is felt at all class levels, but most acutely by low-income populations lacking the resources to purchase private security or buy into gated communities, increasingly the destination of middle-class segments (Caldeira 2002). The Brazil section of the recent World Bank multi-country study *Voices of the Poor* notes that crime, violence and insecurity are the primary concerns of low-income populations, overtaking in importance the customary issues of job creation and the economy (Melo 2002).

Fourth, despite a transition to procedural democracy[3] in most Latin American countries in the 1980s and 1990s and the accompanying formal blueprints

23

for social justice and equality (see, for example, the Brazilian Democratic Constitution of 1988), rarely have the equitable public policies needed to ensure social justice been promulgated (Cardia 2004).[4] Nowhere is this seen more acutely than in the policies for public safety throughout the region, where the trend has been to institute increasingly repressive public safety policies to combat problems whose root causes require social and economic solutions (Ungar 2004).

And finally, the globalized but specifically Latin American phenomenon of illicit trading in drugs and arms has contributed to a dynamic of systemic violence carried out by drugs traffickers and police alike, the latter under the guise of crime-fighting measures. The very porous division of illicit and 'official' violence has created the perverse dynamic of low-income populations often feeling more protected by the 'real' criminals than by the police, their official protectors (Leeds 1996; Alvito 2001).

This chapter will argue that the kinds of violence experienced by low-income urban populations in Rio de Janeiro within the context of the larger trends mentioned above, the absence of adequate social policies and, most importantly, the state's mishandling of public safety policies create a dynamic whereby violence increases exclusion which, in turn, perpetuates the violence. By way of example, the chapter will discuss the failure of Rio's public school system to function in violence-prone areas, the subsequent effect on the economic options for children and youth from these areas, the perverse response of public safety personnel, and the ultimate effect on employment options for adult members of these communities who are excluded from the formal job market or earn less if they are truthful about where they live. Finally, and completing the vicious cycle, the violence once experienced almost exclusively by *favela* residents is now experienced by the city as a whole as the conflicts between drug-related criminal factions and the police are played out on city streets. As the violence increases, the city becomes increasingly polarized and *favela* residents are ever more marginalized. My observations are based on Brazil, and specifically Rio de Janeiro, but what is described is increasingly relevant to other Brazilian cities and to many Latin American urban contexts.[5]

Favela-related violence

The popular image of Rio's violence as portrayed in such recent films as *City of God*, while exaggerating, distorting and decontextualizing the violence, nevertheless focuses on a key symptom of the problem, the alienation of children and adolescents in *favelas* and the attraction to drugs trading for its financial gain, prestige and provision of a sense of identity, community and belonging when these are lacking elsewhere. This attraction feeds into a dynamic of violence that affects the entire city. Virtually all of Rio's 600 *favelas*, which, depending on who is counting, are populated by anything from 1.5 to 2 million people, or a third of the city, have drugs trading organizations that increasingly dominate those communities' economic and political life.

The dominance of drugs trading gangs and the violence associated with their activities grew in the 1980s as cocaine became the drug of choice for the middle class in Brazil as well as in the United States and Europe, leading to Brazil's role as a trans-shipment locus. The relationship between the drugs lord and the *favela* community varies widely from being 'benevolent' to disrespectful and violent. When I first started research on the political impact of drugs trading on local-level democratic organization in the late 1980s and early 1990s, the relationship between *favela* residents' associations and the drugs traders was still a delicate balance, with local associations able to maintain a degree of autonomy (Leeds 1996). Today, that balance has shifted to far greater dominance of local political life by the drugs lords. Drugs trading groups have assumed the role of internal mediator, judge, jury and often punisher of perceived crimes. If any resident is suspected of being a police informer or connected to a rival faction he or she is expelled or even killed (ibid.; Zaluar 2004; Barcellos 2003).[6]

Drugs trading entities, loosely organized into several city-wide factions, have essentially divided the city's *favelas* and their prisons into areas of domination. Those who live in a *favela* dominated by one faction visit a *favela* dominated by a rival faction only at great personal risk. Similarly, Rio's prisons are divided into sections ruled by one faction or another. And those public schools located in or near *favelas* dominated by a particular faction are subject to enormous actual and potential threat by that *favela*'s drugs faction or its rival.

Impact on education

How has this domination affected the quality of schools and incentives for low-income children to remain in school? In parallel with the decline in quality of urban schools of large US cities, the quality and resources of Rio's public schools have declined markedly in the last quarter-century as middle-class children flee public education for private and church-sponsored schools. Teachers of public schools located in or near *favelas* feel under siege and are less inclined or unable to invest time and energy to teaching in trying circumstances. Little effort is made to relate basic education to the social context from which *favela* children come, resulting in high drop-out rates.

Schools have increasingly become a space for contestation between rival drugs factions. Just as no *favela* space can any longer be called neutral vis-à-vis drugs factions, few public schools located in *favela* areas can be considered neutral spaces. This process of intervention of traffickers has dire consequences for quality basic education and the potential of schools to be vehicles for promoting citizenship. Endless examples exist of drugs lords ordering children from *favela* communities to stay away from school if there is to be a threat from a rival faction and of traffickers forcing school officials to make 'agreements' to keep police away from school in exchange for a promise from traffickers not to disrupt school activities.[7]

High drop-out rates, especially marked in the cohort of male *favela* adolescents who have little possibility of employment, create a reserve army for drugs traffickers, with children in that army becoming increasingly younger. They are in fact called *soldados* (soldiers). A 2002 ILO study on children in the Rio drugs trade reports a strong drop in child labour throughout Brazil, and Rio, in particular, has, in the aggregate, one of the lowest rates of child labour in the country, especially in the fifteen-to-seventeen age range. But in *favelas,* in that same fifteen-to-seventeen age range, the rate of child labour is double that of the rest of the metropolitan area, reaching 50 per cent in some *favela* areas. It is this cohort which enters the drugs trade, but that cohort is decreasing in age. The same ILO study noted that the average age for entering drugs trafficking is now in the twelve-to-thirteen range (Souza e Silva and Urani 2002). In 1980 there were 110 convictions among children for drugs trading; in 2001 that figure had risen to 1,584, a 1,340 per cent increase (Dowdney 2003).

Motives for involvement in drugs trading

With less than eight years of primary schooling, getting any kind of job, much less one that pays more than the minimum wage (approximately US$90 per month), is difficult. Those without a complete basic education are not allowed to enlist in military service (often a channel for advancement), are not qualified for more advanced technical/professional courses, and do not have the basic credentials for jobs in banks and employment services (Fernandes 2004). Children and adolescents are pressured to contribute to the family income or are motivated by the desire to consume what is constantly played out in front of them. There is discrimination against all job-seekers who live in *favelas*, but the prejudice is much greater for *favela* youth. Many adults and adolescents give false addresses on job applications to get around the discrimination of potential employers. A 2003 study noted that the salaries of men living in *favelas* were 35 per cent less than those of men in the 'regular' city. Black men in *favelas* earned 50 per cent less than blacks in non-*favela* areas (Queiroz Ribeiro 2002).

Whether because of the absence of a stable and supportive family life or the absence of other effective mechanisms of socialization – school, church, feelings of belonging to a social cohort – or because of the inability to earn an adequate living, youths see 'the life' (drugs trading) as a viable alternative. A common sentiment of the *favela* youth who become involved in drugs trading, documented in a landmark study on children in Rio's drugs trade, is as follows: 'I only got involved in "the life" because I tried to get work and nobody wanted to give me a job, so I said if no one will give me a job I am going into a life of crime ... We try our hardest to get work and they don't want to give us a job so what can we do. We get angry' (Dowdney 2003).

The anger fostered by police misconduct, repression and corruption, combined with the factors mentioned above, frequently serves to push already fragile and marginalized youth into the option of drugs trading. The same young man quoted above notes: ' ... With all the things that we see wrong, what the police are doing ... beating up residents, abusing them ... And so we get angry with this, so I'm telling you that it's the life in the *favela* that makes us angry' (ibid.).

Discrimination and stereotyping by the police and society as a whole frequently lead to the creation of an identity that gang members (in US and Latin American cities in particular) can use to justify their activities (Leeds 1996). It is what anthropologist Luiz Eduardo Soares has called the 'invisibility' of low-income youth, stemming from society's simultaneous discrimination and indifference, its stigmatizing of youth as 'marginal', '*favelado*', an identity-less '*menor*' in the case of street children, whose aberrant behaviour is 'predictable' (Soares 2004). And that 'prediction' frequently results in the self-fulfilling prophecy of that identity-less youth turning to an alternative 'community' and a set of activities that will give him the missing identity. The dynamic of inadequate schools, elevated school drop-out rates for male adolescents and growth in drugs trading coincides with equally high homicide rates for males in the fifteen-to-twenty-four age cohort at both the national and metropolitan (Rio de Janeiro) levels (Fernandes 2004: 266; Mesquita and Loche 2003: 182)

Police and community – negative dialogues

In the period of approximately twenty years since Brazil's process of re-democratization began in the mid-1980s, the sector that has made least progress is criminal justice and, in particular, the police. The democratic constitution of 1988, which, on paper at least, changed virtually all aspects of government, left the police institutions unchanged. One need only read the newspapers of most Brazilian cities, Human Rights Watch and Amnesty International reports or the recently released reports of the United Nations' special envoy on extra-judicial killings to discover that police violence and corruption continue to plague Brazilian society, and low-income populations in particular (Leeds 2006). The police, with few exceptions, have not made the transition from protecting the state, as was their role in the time of dictatorship, to protecting its citizenry, and especially its low-income citizenry, who continue to be treated as the enemy, as was the left during the military regime.

While strategies for controlling drugs trafficking differ from state to state, the standard operations of both the military and civil police of Rio have been to adopt a war-like posture, invading *favelas* in full battle gear with SWAT-style operations, killing innocent people in the cross-fire, and arresting the local drug dealers who, on the way to being booked, are frequently killed for 'resisting arrest' (*auto de resistência*). The annual number of deaths caused by the police in Rio de Janeiro rose vertiginously from 1998 (355) to 2003 (1,195). Of that total, the number of homicides, whether caused by police or not, in the fifteen-to-twenty-four age cohort is even higher. Using the standard ratio of deaths per 100,000 of population, in 2000 alone in Rio the rate was 50 homicides per 100,000 population as a whole, while homicides in the fifteen-to-twenty-four age cohort were 220 per 100,000 population (Ramos and Musumeci 2005). The proportion is greater when black youths of that age cohort are considered separately (Soares and Borges 2004).[8]

Arresting local drugs lords, rather than making a dent in the volume of drugs traffickers, frequently destabilizes the community, allowing an opportunity for rival factions to attempt to take control of the *favela*. There is significant evidence that the police, far from remaining neutral in the factional battles, frequently take sides, giving advantages to one side over the other and gaining financially for their 'assistance'. These turf wars occur with pitched battles exposing the communities to cross-fire from both the drugs factions and the police.[9] Thus, *favela* communities are caught between two forms of violence and there are few attempts to build constructive relationships with the community.

The role of the police in perpetuating drugs trading is a crucial variable in the ongoing dynamic of exclusion–violence–exclusion. Extortion of drugs traders by police is a common practice, as is the blackmailing of innocent residents who are forced to pay off the police in exchange for not being falsely arrested (Souza 1999). Worse is the extortion of youths who are trying to sever involvement with drugs gangs. These youths are known to the police, who continue to extort money from them, forcing them to continue in the trade so they can deliver the money to the police (Dowdney 2003). A cynical but realistic commentary by a Rio drugs trader clearly defines the perceived relationship:

> I don't see a chance for crime to end because, if you do away with crime, you do away with the police ... because it's us who gives money to the police. If it wasn't for drug-trading, the police would earn only their lousy salaries. This way they earn their salaries and the bribes [to look the other way] that we give them ... So drug-trading won't go away any time soon. (Soares et al. 2005: 136)

The net effect of this negative interaction between the police and low-income communities is distrust and disdain of the police by community residents who, while not necessarily in favour of the drug dealers, are even less inclined to cooperate with the police.

A number of recent studies have shown that males of all classes, generally between the ages of eighteen and twenty-five, are subject to discrimination by the police, most commonly in police stops (blitzes). That interaction is clearly racist when male youths of that age cohort are African-Brazilian or perceived by police to live in a *favela*, with the implication that they are drug users or traffickers. A standard phrase heard on police radio transmissions, when referring to black youths is '*elemento suspeito, cor padrão*' (suspect is the 'usual' colour) (Ramos and Musumeci 2005). Middle-class and/or white youths are routinely shaken down for a pay-off while black youths are physically abused (Minayo et al. 1999; Ramos and Musumeci 2005). The understandable disdain of and anger against police by youth is expressed most clearly in the titles and lyrics of Brazil's hip-hop/rap/reggae music groups, reflecting their own experience and that of their prime audience.[10] Perhaps the most expressive of these is by Marcelo Yuka, formerly of the musical group O Rappa: '*Todo camburão tem um pouco de navio negreiro*' – roughly translated as 'all police vans are a bit like a slave ship' (Ramos e Musumeci 2005).

The antipathy generated by police actions, then, serves only to increase the distance between *favelas* and the police, allowing ever greater spaces in which the violence can occur and giving the impression to the organized crime factions that they can act with impunity. When the criminal justice system has attempted to crack down on the activities of drugs traders, whether incarcerated or still at liberty in the *favelas*, the crime factions have retaliated with swift and violent actions affecting both criminal justice officials and common citizens in all parts of the city, leading the press to sensationalize the situation as the 'Colombianization' of Rio.

Analysts of the public safety crises throughout Latin America are quick and correct to point out that the problems and their solutions go beyond the actions of the police. Other segments of the criminal justice system – the prosecutorial and prison sectors – each have their specific structural problems. The lack of a social safety net, deficient social policies and poor employment prospects are critical variables in the public safety dynamic, as mentioned above. But the police are constrained by a specific set of political and administrative factors that impede efforts to create a more citizen-oriented public safety policy. These constraints are particularly evident in Rio de Janeiro.

Political-administrative constraints[11]

Throughout Latin America, and Brazil is no exception, public safety is *the* most important issue of citizen concern in public opinion polls for all class levels. As such, virtually all electoral campaigns produce position papers or platform publications to outline proposed public safety.[12] Rarely, however, are the comprehensive policies outlined in these campaign documents ever implemented. The overtures to public safety improvement are constrained by political/administrative variables that are not unique to Brazil. First and foremost are the political costs of major reform necessary for public safety. In many states and at the federal level, rooting out corrupt police on a scale that would make a difference will inevitably affect standing public officials. Second, police unions and professional associations are consistently opposed to any constitutional change that would dilute their institutional culture. In Brazil the most glaring example is the opposition by police lobbies to amendments to the constitution to allow the unification of the military and civil police forces, the most frequently cited reform measure.

Despite the campaign rhetoric of aspiring politicians, the political costs of carrying out police reform are complicated further by the realization that public safety improvement is dependent on many variables, not just the police. For a particular administration to seriously undertake public safety improvement as a goal is to risk political reputations by claiming responsibility for a reduction in crime, a phenomenon linked to other related variables, mentioned above, such as the prison, prosecutorial and judicial systems and socio-economic variables. The police also use the excuse of the complexity of 'the system' as a way of dodging responsibility for improving performance (Neves et al. 2002).

All too often a particular politician, once in office, opts for the short-term and frequently repressive Band-Aid approach, just to show that progress is being made or that there is a security presence that will make a difference. Governmental response to the perceived public desire for 'get tough' public safety policies in the face of escalating crime rates is a Latin American-wide phenomenon (Ungar 2004). Brazil and Rio are no exceptions. Quick-fix policies tend to appear as elections approach, when incumbents are concerned with responding to a public impatient for crime reduction and hardline policies. Invariably quick fixes lead to an escalation of violence and a worsening of public safety conditions.

And finally, reformers must contend with the inevitable programmatic discontinuities that occur from one political administration to another and within administrations as public safety personnel are replaced mid-stream for a wide variety of reasons. These range from public safety crises for which someone has to accept responsibility – and those in positions of authority are inevitably fired whether or not blame is justified – to the short-sighted view that sufficient progress in crime reduction is not being made and that positive results, however fleeting, require different strategies and personnel.

Of all the structural problems affecting the Rio police, the lack of continuity of policies and practices is perhaps the most damaging of efforts to institute permanent reforms. There are endless examples of programmes created at a particular political moment to, for example, improve the accountability and transparency of the police, sensitize police to issues of domestic violence, improve communications between the different police organizations and create community policing projects that address elevated levels of violence in the *favelas*. It is this last example which is most relevant to the arguments of this chapter.

In September 2000, in the administration of Governor Anthony Garotinho and under the auspices of Public Safety Secretary Luiz Eduardo Soares, a community policing programme was implemented in the *favelas* of Pavão-Pavãozinho and Cantagalo in Rio's middle- and upper-class South Zone. In response to yet another police atrocity – the military police killed five young men in the *favela* in May of that year – resulting in massive street demonstrations by *favela* residents, the Public Safety Secretariat created the Grupo de Policiamento em Áreas Especiais (Police Group for Special Areas) or GPAE. A pilot project inspired by a successsful violence-reduction community policing programme in Boston, Massachusetts, the programme attained significant results in its first year. After first removing fifty police officers who were accused of abuse and violence, and then creating a coalition of government and community organizations to address social issues, the programme was able to reduce to zero the number of deaths in the *favela* and was praised by *favela* residents for creating a new and positive model of police–community relations.

But following the tendency of discontinuity of promising policies and practices, the project lost its focus and purpose when Luiz Eduardo Soares was removed from office by the governor over political differences. The creative and courageous police major (and Soares ally) Antonio Carlos Carballo, who coordinated the project, was removed and given a position that isolated him from similar activities (known in police parlance as 'being put in the refrigerator'). By 2004 the police had returned to business as usual. While GPAE still existed officially, its police personnel had returned to killing *favela* youth with impunity. During that year the police killed four adolescents in the *favela*, three of them in a war-like operation in which the black-clothed, heavily armed police with painted faces first tortured and then killed the youths. Whatever goodwill and efficacy in reducing violence the police had achieved in 2000/01 was wiped out by 2004. There have been recent attempts to restart the programme and expand it to other communities, with as yet limited results.

Police oversight and the lack of political will – costs and consequences

The violence-producing relationship between the police and the *favelas* has existed for several decades and has only been exacerbated with the passage of time. When that relatively small cohort of police began to deviate from its official role as protector of public safety to become enablers of the drugs trade, it started a dynamic that has become difficult to reverse. The consequences of that dynamic have increasingly spread to all sections of the city, with retaliation and counter-retaliation producing increasing episodes of violence (Gay 2005). One of the earliest and best-known examples of this dynamic was the 1993 massacre by the military police of twenty-one innocent residents of the *favela* Vigário Geral in retaliation for a drugs deal with local traffickers that went sour. In the intervening years, police assassinations – usually of black male youth – have become almost routine, as mentioned above. It is only more recently that these acts of violence have begun to affect life outside the *favela* with a certain frequency.

The circumstances that provoke drugs-trafficker retaliation in the city as a whole are varied. There have been a number of episodes in response to the state government's attempt to crack down on the use of mobile phones by imprisoned drugs traffickers or on the inmates' unlimited access to their lawyers. These 'benefits' were part of a long-established system in which prison guards received pay-offs for looking the other way. Retaliation in this case was the assassination of the woman prison director. Other retaliatory responses have been high-powered weapons shot at Rio's City Hall and orders by drugs traffickers, whether in prison or through their 'agents' still at large, to order commerce to shut down on regular city streets, to give just a few examples. The most recent episode, on 29 November 2005, one of the most barbaric to date, was the attack on a city bus by a drugs trafficker resulting in five deaths and many more wounded. The causes were, once again, police extortion of drugs traffickers: the police assigned to one particular *favela* in Rio's North Zone, dissatisfied with their pay-off, began arresting traffickers, thereby depleting their ranks. The drugs lord, not happy with this turn of events, attacked the bus, killing people unknown to him and with no connection to his drugs operation.

The episodes described above are the consequences of a criminal justice system whose potential for oversight has long been compromised by a lack of political will to address abuses by its own personnel. The less the political will, the greater the political costs of fixing the problems of the system when security for all citizens is threatened, as is the case in Rio. The longer the lack of political will persists, the more difficult it is to undo a system and culture of impunity. Of all the efforts at police reform in the past decade, efforts to promote police accountability are usually met with the most hostility, resistance and obstructionism. Of the potential mechanisms of police oversight in Brazil, the most promising, although still highly problematic, is that of the police ombudsman office (*ouvidoria*), created in five states in the mid and late 1990s and now found, in one form or another, in thirteen Brazilian states. The *ouvidorias*, which receive individual complaints from citizens and even from lower-ranking police officers regarding their own institutions, were created to be more effective oversight mechanisms than the long-established police internal affairs offices (*corregedorias*) and the external public prosecutors' offices. With rare exceptions neither of the latter two offices plays an effective police oversight role (Macaulay 2002).

The creation of ombudsman offices is a voluntary act in Brazil. They are instituted in moments of political openness in individual states and with varying degrees of effectiveness. While the first ombudsmen came from the human rights community, broadly speaking, many of their successors have been public prosecutors or otherwise linked to the justice system, with differing degrees of independence. While, in principle, the creation of external oversight vehicles is an essential step in the process of creating a more accountable and effective police service, in reality the conditions of the ombudsmen offices have impeded their effectiveness. Their autonomy has been limited by several factors: 1) scarce financial resources; 2) their physical locations within the offices of their state secretariats of public safety, which calls into question their independence; 3) their appointments being ultimately made by the governor of their states, thus creating political linkages that limit autonomy; and 4) their lack of subpoena and independent investigative power (Lemgruber et al. 2003).

These problematic institutional arrangements are compounded by poor or non-existent records kept by police and coroners' offices on potential police abuse. For example, a consistent finding of police researchers is the mislabelling in police reports of encounters with victims in which torture or death occurs. The category 'bodily harm' (*lesão corporal*) frequently hides occurrences of torture or death by excessive force, and 'resisting arrest' is often found as the explanation for torture or death when, in fact, deliberate excessive force was employed (Cano 1997). Even if adequate resources and information were available, the resolution of individual cases would do nothing to change public safety policy in a more comprehensive way. As Rio's first police ombudsperson, Julita Lemgruber, has noted, focusing on the 'bad apples' does little to change the structure, administration and culture of police, which are the larger causal factors (Lemgruber et al. 2003).[13]

Conclusions

This chapter has attempted to trace a series of interrelated social, economic and political problems which, without adequate solution, had led the city of Rio de Janeiro to experience an escalating rate of violence, exacerbating class divisions and further marginalizing its significant low-income communities. Within the context of larger structural variables that are characteristic of most large cities in developing countries, Rio's particular characteristics – its role as a trans-shipment locus for lucrative illicit drugs, its geographic design, its structure of semi-organized criminal factions, its poor-quality public education and its intransigent public safety policy – have produced a quagmire of violence begetting violence. As has been shown in examples from the recent past, when political will exists to address deficient public policies, public safety in particular, the potential for breaking the cycle of violence becomes apparent. The overriding question remains why, in the face of damage to its social, economic and political fabric and image, Rio city and state officials continue to opt for ineffectual and/or destructive policies.

Notes

1 See, for example, Ward et al. (2004).

2 There is, by now, a vast literature in Latin America on urban violence. For the more helpful overviews see Moser and McIlwaine (2004), especially ch. 1; Koonings and Kruijt (2004); and Morrison et al. (2003).

3 Procedural democratic practices are defined here as those that support free speech, open elections, freedom of association and the unhindered functioning of political parties. These practices are distinct from the notion of substantive democracy which argues that equality of opportunity should be afforded all segments of the population through the right to quality education, health and housing and a judicial and public safety system which is equally respectful to all.

4 Nancy Cardia (2004) convincingly explores the relation between violence and the lack of access to substantive democratic rights such as employment and basic urban services in metropolitan São Paulo.

5 The kind of drug-related violence that was almost exclusively the domain of Rio de Janeiro for twenty-five years is now found, to one degree or another, in metropolitan areas throughout the country. For ethnographic description of gang and drug-related activities in Brasilia, São Paulo, the southern cities of Porto Alegre, Joinville, Curitiba and the north/north-eastern cities of Belem, Aracajú and João Pessoa, see Soares et al. (2005).

6 The number of legitimate *favela* leaders assassinated has grown significantly in recent years. Between 1987 and 1995 the number of deaths as reported by the Federação de Favelas de Estado do Rio de Janeiro between 1987 and 1995 was twenty-five (Leeds 1996). Zaluar (2004) reports 800 community leaders murdered, expelled or co-opted between 1992 and 2001. It is not known how many were murdered.

7 The most vivid description of this phenomenon in Rio de Janeiro may be found in Guimarães (1998: ch. 1). For a more general discussion of school violence in the country, see Abramovay and Rua (2002).

8 Siliva Ramos makes a further distinction by analysing homicide rates per 100,000 by specific areas of the municipality of Rio de Janeiro, and notes that the poorest regions of the city register homicide rates of 84 per 100,000 population while the city's richest areas register rates of 4.7 to 10 per 100,000.

9 For the clearest examination of this issue see the superb documentary by film-maker João Salles, *Notícias de uma guerra particular*, and the equally superb journalistic ethnography, *Abusado* by Caco Barcellos, both focusing on the Favela Santa Marta in Rio's South Zone.

10 See, for example, 'Polícia' by the group Titãs; 'Diário de um détente' by Os Racionais; and 'Tribunal da Rua' by O Rappa (Ramos e Musumeci 2005).

11 For more general discussions of constraints to police reform see Leeds (2006) and Beato et al. (forthcoming).

12 The election campaigns for Anthony Garotinho (governor of Rio de Janeiro in 1998) and Luiz Inacio Lula da Silva (president of Brazil in 2002) both produced books on their prospective public safety policies, ghost-written by Luiz Eduardo Soares, who would become the responsible public safety secretary in both cases. After Soares left both offices, his innovative plans were all but abandoned.

13 For the political constraints on undertaking police accountability measures in any significant way, see Luiz Eduardo Soares's memoir recounting his fifteen months as Secretary of Public Safety of Rio, especially pp. 413–18 (Soares 2000).

3 | Mexico City

WIL PANSTERS AND HECTOR CASTILLO BERTHIER*

Violence as fact and phantom

Pointing his finger at two small spots on his neck, the Mexico City taxi driver recounted how a passenger had attacked him with an iron peg three weeks earlier. The thief left the taxi with the equivalent of three dollars. The driver did not report the robbery and was lucky he didn't suffer a more serious injury.[1] Most inhabitants of contemporary Mexico City are able to tell how they themselves, a family member or a friend have been the victim of some form of delinquent behaviour (assault, robbery, kidnapping, extortion, etc.). This simple example also contains two important clues about insecurity and violence in the metropolitan area: the significance of the poor stealing from the poor, and the fact that much, some would say most, of what actually goes on does not make it into the official statistics.

In the last ten years, insecurity and violence have become a hotly debated and contested issue in the daily lives of those who reside in the crowded and contaminated Valley of Mexico. This chapter was written at a time of growing public concern about mostly drug-related executions and assassinations throughout the country. In the spring and summer of 2005 newspapers reported new cases almost on a daily basis, while authorities were on the defensive. Although most of the drug-related crime occurs in the northern states, in Mexico City a debate raged about a publicity campaign about insecurity that suggested that Mexico had become a 'city of fear'. The line that separates factual violence and its perception is increasingly hard to identify.

The anxieties about violence and insecurity, however, as well as the phenomena themselves, have meanings that go beyond their sociological referents. It therefore seems reasonable to also look at violence and insecurity as a 'phantom' that wanders the metropolis. First, the phantom of violence is associated with changing urban lifestyles. A widespread feeling of insecurity causes people to restrict their circulation in public spaces and avoid leaving their homes at night or visiting certain areas. Instead, people withdraw behind closed doors and move in(to) private spaces. As a result, the interaction with 'others' from different social backgrounds diminishes and sociabilities that may arise from spontaneous encounters in public spaces are discouraged.

Groups and social classes seek refuge among peers, and a sense of suspicion towards others becomes generalized. Urban design changes as gated neighbourhoods and guarded apartment complexes proliferate. Spending on insurance, private security and protection systems increases. Commercial activities tend to concentrate in large malls protected against assaults and robberies. Violence thus stimulates changes in urban design, daily life and the perception and valorization of insecurity, favouring security above contact. Second, the phantom of violence generalizes social segregation and stigmatization. Young, low-income males represent the possibility of aggression or assault. Socio-economic and age- and gender-specific characteristics convert the individual into a negatively valued prototype. The phantom generalizes and constructs an archetype, that of the male juvenile delinquent. Third, the phantom of violence seems to replace the theme of social conflict. It is no coincidence that profound discursive and ideological shifts have made the theme of social (in)justice ever more muffled, whereas that of penal justice can be heard everywhere. Of course, citizen perceptions of the failures of justice are justified by corruption, impunity, institutionalized fraud and police abuse. Fourth, together with the alarm about drugs, the phantom of violence crystallizes the fears of neo-liberal modernization. Anxieties stemming from the fragmentation of space, the weakening of social cohesion and the fractures in public and private morality relocate towards objects suitable for speculation and conjecture: urban violence and the flood of drugs. Finally, the phantom of violence is exploited and inflated by the media. In the hands of reporters, violence becomes the centre of the news and turns into a spectacle that nourishes the viewer's fears of aggression and vulnerability. No wonder that, in the domain of politics and electoral competition, the phantom of violence gives rise to calls for exceptional measures such as zero-tolerance policing.[2] In sum, the phantom of violence symbolically shores up the disciplining of society in contemporary Mexico City.

In this chapter we look at violence and insecurity from different angles. First, we provide some basic information about the sociology, geography and politics of the metropolis. Second, we map the phenomena of insecurity and violence in the capital and relate our findings to the broader sociology of the city. What do the statistics of crime, insecurity and violence tell us about the situation, and how can these be related to processes of exclusion, poverty and informalization? We pay special attention to the problem of drugs. In this section we also look at some actors of violence (police and youth gangs). Third, we examine the consequences and responses of different urban actors to an increasingly complex problem. How do ordinary citizens perceive the

Mexico City

issues of insecurity, crime and violence? How can the policies of the local government that attempt to resolve or diminish the problem be qualified? What strategies are being employed by different sections of civil society? In this context we will look at the practice and politics of lynching.

Metropolitan structure and security governance

Mexico City's size is not easy to determine: the question of where the city starts and where it ends is by no means clear cut. As a result, estimates about the population size of the city vary. In general terms, Mexico City can be divided into two parts: the Federal District (Distrito Federal; DF) and the surrounding urban area that forms part of the State of Mexico (Estado de México), one of Mexico's thirty-one federal states which surrounds the Federal District as a ring. The metropolitan area contains almost 18 million people.[3] The city's most dramatic growth occurred between 1960 and 1980, when the population grew from over 5 million to almost 15 million. The territorial boundaries of the metropolitan area are pushing farther and farther into the State of Mexico. Today, the metropolitan area – we will use the term Mexico City Metropolitan Area (MCMA) in this chapter – covers almost 3,000 square kilometres and constitutes, in terms of its sheer physical and human dimensions, an enormous 'social laboratory' full of intensity and contrasts. In the Mexican capital the embarrassing opulence of some social sectors shares an urban space with depressing neighbourhoods without water and other services, locked up in ravines and creeping up against steep hillsides. It is a place with overwhelming public and private corruption in all social sectors, which has grown out of deficient urban planning, leading to ever widening 'circles of misery', both as a result of natural demographic growth and the continued arrival of migrants. It is a place of sharp contrasts: the Federal District, even with its multiple poor *barrios*, has a highly developed urban infrastructure and is the focus of economic, political and commercial power. The wider metropolitan area, on the other hand, contains wholly urbanized zones with high-tech malls, apartment complexes and fancy office buildings, but also irregular settlements, overcrowded proletarian neighbourhoods, a lack of services, unpaved streets, entire areas without drinking water, webs of cables that rob some of the city's electricity, delinquency, malnutrition, and poorly dressed children who roam the dusty roads of what was once a lake. Despite geographical, social, political and administrative divisions – the last of which will be dealt with below – the city still functions as an interconnected whole. In daily life administrative boundaries hardly matter. As a consequence, the contradictions between modernity and marginality are everywhere, as are the social problems that come with them, seemingly impossible to resolve. They have become part of an urban landscape that is grim and gloomy as well as effervescent and creative. All this constitutes Mexico City.[4]

The sheer size of the mega-city can give some idea of the complexities of governance and administration that affect the lives of millions every day in terms of housing, transport, labour markets and security. The Federal District is divided into sixteen so-called *delegaciones* or delegations, each of which is headed by a *delegado*. The surrounding urban area nowadays consists of thirty-five different municipalities, each with its own chosen mayor, who in their turn have to deal with the governor of the State of Mexico.[5] Since the Federal District is the official seat of the federal executive, legislative and judicial powers, the federation has constitutional powers in the capital as well. For many years, the citizens of the Federal District did not enjoy the same political rights as other Mexicans, since they were unable to elect the authorities of their city. This changed in 1997, as the result of negotiations between the ruling elite and the opposition parties that had gradually been opening up the political and electoral system. The mayor as well as the *delegados* were then elected directly by the citizens in a overwhelming victory for opposition leader Cuauhtémoc Cárdenas of the centre-left PRD. The PRD has retained power ever since. The situation became more complex in 2000, when the PRI candidate for the presidency was defeated by Vicente Fox of the right-wing PAN. This created the following political panorama in the Mexico City metropolitan area: the federal government, with substantial political interests in the capital (see below), is in the hands of the PAN, the government of the Federal District is in the hands of the PRD (as are most *delegaciones*), while the government of the State of Mexico and most of its municipalities is in the hands of the PRI.[6] This complicated situation became highly politicized in 2004 and early 2005 when partisan political rivalries between incompatible personalities intensified to such a degree that they led to an open conflict between the mayor of Mexico City, Andrés Manuel López Obrador, President Fox and major interests in the PRI, eventually leading to a process of *desafuero* (impeachment) in April 2005.

Tense political relations between different administrative levels and political actors will certainly not contribute to resolving the immense problems of the metropolitan area. There are organizational divisions within security governance. The system consists of a wide variety of police corporations. Both citizens and authorities in the MCMA area have to deal with federal police corporations, those of the DF as well as municipal police forces and the state police of the State of Mexico. To complicate matters further, the police forces

39

of the federation and the DF are each divided into the Preventive Police and the Judicial Police. Finally, there is the Policía Bancaria e Industrial, a private force hired by the government of the DF, as well as the Policía Auxiliar, a semi-private corporation basically in charge of safeguarding buildings. According to a recent review of the structure and cost of the metropolitan police forces, there are approximately 110,000 police officers working in the metropolitan area. Moreover, and in response to the state's failure to provide security, there are hundreds of companies active in the business of private security. The country as a whole holds third place worldwide in terms of the purchase of security equipment (Reames 2003: 9). A study prepared for the Asamblea Legislativa of the DF in early 2004 reports over six hundred registered companies in the DF alone, employing more than 21,000 people.

The complexity of the security system derives not only from territorial and administrative divisions, but from also from certain legal distinctions. Most important in this context is a differentiation according to type of criminal offence. Certain offences, such as those related to drugs, are so-called federal offences and can thus be handled only by federal police forces. As we will show later, this legal prerogative creates particular problems of coordination between police corporations. There is a complicated distribution of political responsibilities. Since the DF is the official seat of the federal authorities, tradition has it that the federal executive has the authority to appoint two key figures in the domain of security of the city government: the secretary of public security as well as attorney general of the DF. Since 1997, when the mayor of the DF was elected by popular vote, these appointments by the president follow the recommendation of the elected mayor. Nevertheless, the president can still dismiss the secretary, as happened at the end of 2004.

Patterns and actors of insecurity and violence

Historical patterns of crime Major features of crime in the MCMA during the twentieth century can be distinguished. First, corruption within the security forces and their involvement with criminals have lowered the cost of transgressing the law and have discouraged victims from denouncing crime. For decades, the security forces have been responsible for measuring actual crime rates in the city, and hence combating crime. In recent years this has led to a debate about the so-called 'dark numbers' of crime. Second, the police and the judiciary have throughout the century been perceived by the citizenry as major participants in crime, harassment and violence, rather than as protectors. The different branches of the police and the judiciary enjoy extremely low rates of legitimacy, because they are widely perceived to be involved in different kinds of crime. Throughout the last century there was evidence of the involvement of the police forces and other security agencies in a range of illegal activities such as graft, gambling, prostitution, smuggling and drug trafficking. Third, domestic violence, particularly against women, has been a persistent phenomenon but has also largely remained invisible. Fourth, urban communities have dealt with crime and violence through informal mechanisms and negotiations (Piccato 2003).[7] More recent data point to an additional feature, i.e. the fact that the historical dynamics of crime and violence have a strong correlation with economic cycles.

Recent trends and components of crime Official statistics on crime and violence in the MCMA are generally considered untrustworthy (Arango Durán 2003, 2004; Jiménez Ornelas 2003; Alvarado 2002). The most important factor that accounts for unreliable statistics is that government institutions are able to provide information only about crimes that are actually reported to the police and processed by the judicial system. Hence, 'real' crime rates can only be estimated if unreported crimes are taken into consideration. In recent years, several independent surveys have been undertaken and have shifted attention to the perception and subjective experience of (in)security (González Placencia and Rodríguez Una 2001; González Placencia 2002).[8] These have consistently stressed that almost three out of four affected citizens do not report the crime. Notwithstanding the fact that the discrepancy between official statistics and independent survey results is vast, the trends they show are similar (Alvarado 2002: 8). With this in mind we now turn to a more detailed and longitudinal analysis of criminal offences in the Federal District. From the following data two general conclusions can be drawn.

The first is that the overwhelming majority of criminal offences in the Federal District consist of mugging, robbery, theft and burglary. Taken together they account for 82 per cent of all offences registered by the Office of the Attorney General in 2002. This category also includes attacks on and hijacking of public transport minivans, whereby criminals steal possessions from passengers. This criminal activity underlines the fact that the poor are often involved in stealing from other poor people.

The second general conclusion refers to the trend that emerges from the data. In the mid-1990s, the Federal District witnessed a dramatic increase in all types of crime (except homicides), leading one scholar to speak of an '*epidemia delictiva*' (Alvarado 2000: 410; see also Lozano et al. 2000). This can mostly be explained by the advent and deepening of the economic crisis that hit Mexico in the immediate aftermath of the Salinas presidency (1988–94).

41

TABLE 3.1 Principal criminal offences in the Federal District, 1993–2002, absolute numbers and (percentages)

	1993	1994	1995	1996	1997	1998	1999	2000	2001	2002
Theft and mugging	12,952 (18.6)	16,828 (17.7)	23,530 (16.05)	29,397 (17.4)	34,270 (20.2)	42,725 (26.51)	49,493 (30.98)	24,619 (20.46)	21,587 (19.91)	20,960 (20.36)
Robberies in public transport	5,199 (7.5)	10,412 (10.92)	17,752 (12.11)	28,589 (16.92)	23,085 (13.6)	19,417 (12.05)	16,039 (10.04)	11,861 (9.86)	12,041 (11.11)	10,150 (9.86)
Car theft	19,328 (27.7)	29,342 (30.78)	56,498 (38.53)	57,132 (33.81)	58,480 (34.46)	47,110 (29.23)	44,776 (28.03)	43,644 (36.27)	38,336 (35.36)	34.475 (33.49)
Burglary (residential)	5,416 (7.8)	5,505 (5.78)	7,745 (5.28)	8,706 (5.15)	8,551 (5.04)	8,387 (5.2)	8,225 (5.15)	6,334 (5.26)	6,906 (6.37)	6,763 (6.57)
Burglary (business)	12,031 (17.3)	15,062 (15.8)	19,862 (13.55)	20,598 (12.19)	18,580 (10.95)	16,885 (10.48)	15,075 (9.44)	12,418 (10.32)	12,585 (11.61)	12,438 (12.08)
Homicide	921 (1.3)	1,099 (1.15)	1,204 (0.82)	1,076 (0.64)	977 (0.58)	947 (0.59)	880 (0.55)	709 (0.59)	811 (0.75)	748 (0.73)
Acts of violence	12,543 (18.0)	15,776 (16.55)	18,753 (12.79)	22,065 (13.06)	24,292 (14.32)	24,495 (15.2)	23,926 (14.98)	19,234 (15.98)	14,950 (13.79)	16,116 (15.65)
Rape	1,222 (1.8)	1,299 (1.36)	1,289 (0.88)	1,420 (0.84)	1,448 (0.85)	1,226 (0.76)	1,355 (0.85)	1,511 (1.26)	1,202 (1.11)	1,298 (1.26)
Total	69,612	95,323	146,633	168,983	169,683	161,192	159,769	120,330	108,418	102,948

Source: Authors' elaboration of Procuraduría General de Justicia del Distrito Federal, *Indices Delictivos del Distrito Federal*, 9 December 2003; Procuraduría General de Justicia del Distrito Federal, *Indices Delictivos del Distrito Federal, Resumen Ejecutivo de las Actividades de la PGJDF 2004*, 17 January 2005.

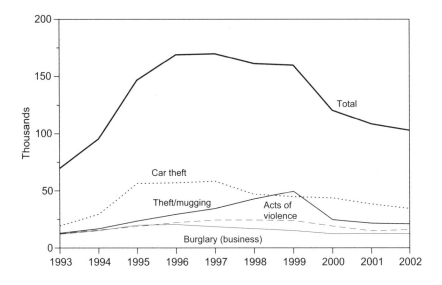

Figure 3.1 Trends of total and selected criminal offences in the Federal District, 1993–2002 (absolute numbers) (*Source*: authors' elaboration of Table 3.1)

Equally, a broader study of Mexico City between 1975 and 1999 has shown the statistical relationship between economic crisis and crime rates. The delinquency trend shows two large surges that correspond to the two most important economic crises of the country after 1945, the debt crisis of 1982 and the peso crisis of 1994/95 (Soberón et al 2003). Table 3.1 demonstrates how reported crimes rose spectacularly from almost 70,000 in 1993 to almost 170,000 in 1997, an increase of over 140 per cent. The numbers remained high for a few more years and then started to decline again. They never returned, however, to the levels of crime seen before the outbreak of the peso crisis.

Drugs It is generally assumed that the imprisonment of several top drug barons in recent years has resulted in fierce and lethal struggles between Mexico's different drug cartels for control of the country's different regions. It has been reported that during the first seven months of 2005 approximately eight hundred people were assassinated as a consequence of the struggle for territorial control in the drug business.[9] The overwhelming majority of these killings have taken place in the northern states of Sinaloa (core region of the cartel of Sinaloa), Tamaulipas (base of the Gulf cartel), Baja California and Chihuahua. In the Federal District and the adjacent State of Mexico twenty-seven executions have been related to drug trafficking. While the big Mexican cartels do not appear to operate primarily from the nation's capital (although some leading drug lords are believed to run their business from a maximum-security prison in the capital), drugs have become a growing concern for the citizens of Mexico City in recent years, mainly because of increased consumption. A poll conducted by the newspaper *Reforma* in April 2004, a so-called victimization study, found that 43 per cent of those interviewed felt that small-scale sale of drugs (*narcomenudeo*) had become common in their neighbourhoods.[10]

This brings us to the question of what the authorities have done to combat the spread of *narcomenudeo*. The key issue here is the absence of an integrated governmental strategy. Since drug-related crimes are legally the responsibility of federal agencies, local police forces, which are often closer to developments in the working-class neighbourhoods, are increasingly frustrated about their inability to act and search houses when they receive complaints or tips. For example, when the Ministry of Public Security of the Federal District elaborated the 'delinquency map' that identified over two thousand drug distribution points, it could only hand the information over to the federal authorities and hope that they would take action.[11] Over the last year, officials and politicians have met time and again to discuss two crucial questions: first, a legal reform that will enable state and municipal police forces to intervene in drug-related crime perpetrated by the large-scale (inter)national cartels, thus ending the monopoly of federal police forces in this branch of crime. Second, local and federal authorities have attempted to overcome the legal and organizational fragmentation of the Mexico City law enforcement agencies by putting together special inter-institutional police units, consisting of police officers from federal, state-level and municipal forces. Several experimental task forces have been organized, but it remains to be seen whether the long history of political rivalries between different government levels as well as the long and often violent conflicts between different police forces can be overcome. Cynical observers will probably argue that the measure will only serve to bring more actors into the profitable drug business, and hence trigger more violence. After all, the Mexico City police forces certainly cannot boast a clean record.

Police Direct involvement in criminal practices and corruption on the part of those officially involved in protection, crime prevention and punishment, and the related problem of impunity, have themselves become crime factors. For decades, urban communities managed to control crime and violence through negotiations between criminals, police forces, the judiciary, victims and neighbourhood leaders. Since the 1970s, however, this modus vivendi has increasingly been undermined by the perceived involvement of the police in the expansion of corruption, violence and drug trafficking (Piccato 2003: 2, 21). This broadly coincided with the regime of the Federal District police chief Arturo Durazo, one of the most infamous police officials in the modern history of the city. An old friend of José López Portillo, who assumed the presidency in 1976, he was appointed chief of police and was protected until 1982, when a discredited and equally corrupt López Portillo left office. Durazo was later prosecuted and jailed. According to Piccato, Durazo's tenure as police chief marks a 'historic shift because ... it systematized longstanding connections between the Federal District's police and diverse illegal businesses. The resulting "criminal organization" in the institution's ranks survived as "la Hermandad"', a secret network of police officials involved in illegal activities (ibid.: 6–7). López-Montiel has argued that the brotherhood works as a complex chain of protection and corruption that guarantees impunity (2000: 85). Although the existence of the 'Hermandad' is surrounded by myth and speculation, it is still believed to exist. This network, with its corresponding organizational culture, is supposed to be governed by a set of strict codes of conduct and loyalties and by the organized distribution of spoils. The absence of effective mechanisms of control and accountability within the police forces further enhances the opportunities for discretionary action.[12]

Abusive behaviour on the part of the metropolitan police forces takes various forms. Torture and the use of excessive force are applied as techniques of investigation and thus as ways to 'resolve' specific cases or as ways of punishing deviant behaviour. In other cases they have been employed to extract financial benefits from victims.[13] A rent is also obtained through paid protection. Most formal businesses (such as restaurants, bars, bakeries and cinemas) pay money directly to the police chief of a certain urban sector (each *delegación* is made up of four sectors). Some of the money goes up the command chain, some down, and the rest remains with the sector chiefs themselves. This amounts to armed protection of private interests by a public institution in exchange for cash payment. A second source of income is cover-up operations, whereby police officers extract money from criminals and people engaged in illegal activities, who are either protected from prosecution or let off the hook. Evidently, by its very nature, this involves the police in informal and illegal activities, such as robberies and contraband. As a large part of Mexico City's population is involved in the grey zone of the informal and illegal economy, this provides ample rent-seeking opportunities for the police. One former top member of the Cárdenas administration of the Federal District recalled that one night he received a phone call about several trucks entering the neighbourhood of Tepito, probably full of contraband, but protected by an escort of the federal judicial police, which prevented him from taking action.[14] The area around Tepito is one of the city's most important hot spots, both in terms of population movement and because of the juxtaposition of banks, government offices, museums and law firms and poor inner-city slums, which makes it an attractive place for criminal activities. Statistics show that in 2003 the central neighbourhood of Mexico City had by far the highest crime rates.[15] This part of the city is thus also a place where the police are found to be involved in numerous illegal and criminal activities. A third source of income is the direct involvement of police officers in criminal activities, such as kidnapping, extortion and drug trafficking. Recently revealed confidential reports about the Federal Preventive Police, the national force that was founded in the 1990s, mention the existence of a so-called 'Hermandad del Polvo Blanco' (White Powder Brotherhood), which protects drug traffickers and is directly involved in the business. These reports confirm the rent-seeking nature of policing, and mentioned the case of the 'sale' of the position of police commander of Mexico City's international airport for $3.5 million.[16] One scholar has even suggested that Mexican security and law enforcement agencies are driven by a 'predatory ethic' that makes them key actors in organized crime (Gómez-Cespedes 1999). The interconnections between the state and organized crime thus run through the security forces and the judiciary system (Shelley 2001). Indeed, the Mexican police rank among the institutions that enjoy the lowest levels of legitimacy and public trust, factors that in turn reinforce organizational tendencies of corporate solidarity and secrecy (Azaola 2004).

Youth gangs In 2000 almost 37.5 per cent of the population of the DF was between ten and twenty-nine years old, forming a legion of more than 3.2 million youngsters.[17] Mexico City's youngsters are born and grow up in highly distinct socio-economic and cultural contexts, which mark their later development in significant ways. The theme of juvenile delinquency is a hotly debated issue among criminologists and sociologists. Youth gangs employ slogans such as 'for the *barrio* I was born, for the *barrio* I will die' and 'the law is the enemy', and assume names like La Vida Loca, Blood for Blood, Denfo du Barrio (Die for the Barrio) and MM (Mexican Mafia). Gang members wear distinctive clothing (identifiable only to members) and use tattoos as symbols of identity (for example, tears below the eyes that indicate the number of killings they have perpetrated). These gangs are in fact juvenile 'self-defence' organizations operating in 'enemy territory', where being a poor young man implies paying a high price of discrimination; where the only exit from marginality appears to be breaking the law; where social and economic violence is confronted with more violence; where '*la vida no vale nada*' (life is worthless), and death has started to be a lucrative business.

Different forces in the metropolis provide the social basis allowing these gangs to emerge. For many, schools no longer function as channels of social ~~*schools*~~ mobility and hence these youngsters develop survival strategies in informal or openly delinquent activities. The family, the institution where values of solidarity and community were traditionally transmitted, is under increasing pressure; single-parent households struggle for economic survival and push the young on to the streets to work – to what some in Mexico City call the '*la universidad de la vida*' (the university of life). Abuse, violence and alcoholism at home add another dimension to the problem. The labour market, with its dramatic imbalance between supply and demand, excludes large groups of youngsters from formal employment and integration. Finally, different sources of (public) authority have been seriously undermined, with the possible exception of the Church. The most visible face of authority for many of these youngsters is the police.

Youth gangs have been an important characteristic of criminality in Mexico City for a long time, but have become particularly notorious since the 1970s, when the *chavos banda* from the poor neighbourhoods came to represent a threat of violence (Piccato 2003: 18). Nowadays, two groups in particular merit mention: the *cholos* and the *maras*, both of which are linked in different ways to violence and insecurity. The *cholos* find their origins among young migrants to the USA, where they developed distinctive cultural practices and forms of identity and where they became involved in different forms of criminality and violence. From there the *cholo* phenomenon migrated back to Mexico, first to the large urban centres along the US–Mexican border and then southwards. Currently, they are involved in drug trafficking and theft. They are also involved in a bitter struggle for territorial control with the *maras*, who originated from the Salvadorean community in Los Angeles, migrated back to El Salvador and from there to Mexico and other parts of Central America. One insider estimated that there are around 1,300 *maras* in Mexico City, divided into seven gangs, and that the city had seen nothing yet (Castillo Berthier 2005).

Governmental and societal responses and strategies

As the situation and the perception of violence and crime unfold, different actors in the city respond to them. The government, the business community, political parties, social organizations, the media and ordinary citizens formu-

47

late proposals and develop strategies to confront the problem. In this section we will look at some of the strategies and actions undertaken by different players in metropolitan society. First we look at some key initiatives taken by the local government since the mid-1990s. Then we briefly focus on an effort by organized civil society to influence the agenda. Finally, we examine one of the perverse consequences of the situation of insecurity, impunity and violence in Mexico City, when poor and frustrated ordinary citizens take the law into their own hands.

Local government: militarization and zero tolerance Since the mid-1990s, the authorities have launched several projects to improve the security situation, sometimes with draconian measures. Given that the police forces have for long had a reputation for being corrupt, undisciplined, unprofessional and technically incompetent, several projects have focused on their reform. This is the context in which the authorities decided to militarize the Mexico City police, as had occurred before elsewhere in Mexico and in combating drug trafficking (O'Day 2001).

In June 1996, at the height of the post peso-crisis upsurge in crime, General Salgado Cordero, still an active member of the Mexican army, was appointed head of police. The new chief pledged to restructure the police and reduce crime and corruption. To that end he immediately replaced 150 high- and middle-level police officers with army personnel. He also sent an entire division of policemen to a military training camp, using lack of professionalism as justification, and replaced them with military police (López-Montiel 2000: 83). From the beginning, the militarization project experienced problems. First, rivalries with the police forces, who were unwilling to surrender their command, sometimes led to overt struggles for control. It was thus only a question of time until the effectiveness of the plan was questioned. The rivalries also had a material basis: soldiers are better paid, enjoy better fringe benefits and have better arms.[18]

Second, the experience laid bare the fact that the operational logic of the military is distinct from that of policing. From the start of the project, critics observed that army officers act according to rules and routines that are not appropriate for normal police work (ibid.: 87). Several incidents caused by military-type police operations in Mexico City upset both the authorities and the public. Most important in this respect were violent police raids, whereby large groups of officers would go into certain neighbourhoods where houses and individuals would be searched for drugs, weapons and stolen goods.

General Salgado left the police force at the end of 1997, when the PRD government of Cuauhtémoc Cárdenas took over. The latter appointed a retired army officer as chief of police, but he too was fired after a year and replaced by a civilian. The military organization of the Mexico City police was dismantled, while officers who had been sacked in previous years were readmitted to the force. Militarizing the police failed because of a complex set of interrelated factors: the social, organizational and cultural rivalries were intense and hence the two were unable and unwilling to cooperate, large political and economic interests were at stake, and the military lacked policing abilities. The failure is also explained by popular discontent, not only because of the harsh methods, but also because of the fact that citizens prefer to work out 'arrangements' with the police, something that is more difficult with the army.[19] López-Montiel's overall conclusion is gloomy: 'it does not matter whether the chief of police is military or civilian; police officers and corrupt organizations have shown the ability to adapt to either ... [and] ... corrupt practices are not abandoned under any kind of government' (ibid.: 89).

Although official statistics show a gradual decline in delinquency since the late 1990s, the authorities have remained under pressure to develop new initiatives aimed at reducing crime. A major initiative of the government of López Obrador (2000–06) was geared towards increasing the coordination of crime prevention, policing and the procurement of justice. This translated into an effort to territorialize the functions of the different agencies and actors involved in matters of (in)security. The objective was an integral approach to crime reduction that would eliminate impunity, attack delinquency, promote social and economic development and improve the relationship between law enforcement agencies and the general public. It involved the Ministry of Public Security and the attorney general of the Federal District as well as the ministries of education and health. The city was divided into seventy so-called Territorial Coordinations on the basis of demographic information, incidence of delinquency, the distribution of police precincts, etc. They were to function as organizational platforms for collaboration between various government agencies, with citizen participation. Although this project showed several positive elements, despite its bureaucratic complexity, it was soon overtaken by a new major plan, most likely because the authorities were under political pressure to launch more pronounced and visible measures.

Early in 2003, López Obrador contracted the former mayor of New York, Rudolph Giuliani, to make an analysis of the situation in Mexico City and formulate recommendations. The hope was that the successful application of the policy of 'zero tolerance' in the Big Apple could be repeated in Mexico. Later that year the Giuliani team produced a document with almost 150 recommendations, which were all hastily accepted by the Ministry of Public Security of the Federal District.[20] Not even the simplest infraction of the law would be tolerated, since permissive behaviour would only lead to worse, hence the idea of zero tolerance. Although no one doubted the report's basic concern – to do something about the profound institutional weakness of the police force – it was critically received in Mexico City by numerous observers.[21] A particular measure proposed in the Giuliani report in this respect provoked widespread criticism, since it suggested the criminalization of the thousands of young boys who work on the streets of Mexico City as '*franeleros*' and '*limpia-parabrisas*' (windscreen washers). A key consequence of Mexico's highly unequal socio-economic system, the extensive informal sector, in which a large part of the city's population struggles for survival, is thus made an object of policing. This issue points to a broader critique that questioned the applicability of the New York model to a city that is socio-economically, politically and legally highly different. Arroyo (2003) has identified serious obstacles to a successful introduction of the philosophy and mechanics of zero tolerance. Basically, Giuliani's approach to the problem of crime is based on the idea that the consequences of social disorder and disobeying the law should be fought with vigorous police action. In Mexico City, however, the police service itself should be held partly responsible for widespread impunity and corruption and thus for a broadly felt sense of insecurity, disorder and a deteriorating quality of life. Hence, Arroyo concludes that the adoption of Giuliani's project is flawed from conception, since the authorities adopted a solution before they knew the problem. The introduction of zero tolerance in New York was a political project based on criminological knowledge, while in Mexico it could only be a political banner (ibid.: 1).

Civic activism Twenty years ago, Mexico City experienced a serious earthquake that killed thousands of people and destroyed large buildings in the centre of the city. In the face of governmental paralysis and failure to act quickly in the ensuing chaos, large groups of citizens themselves took to the streets and organized rescue activities. The civic activism in the aftermath of the 1985 earthquake later consolidated into a strong network of neighbourhood organizations that has been instrumental in bringing about significant changes in Mexico's political system. Despite the fact that insecurity and urban violence as well as discontent about the inability of the government to combat them are the primary sources of concern among today's metropolitan's citizens, they have not (yet) produced comparable sustained civic organizational efforts. What exists on the ground has, moreover, largely emerged in a dependent relation with the state, since the municipal government itself took the lead in creating new relationships with neighbourhoods. In 1999, the people of the Federal District for the first time elected the members of around 1,350 neighbourhood committees, which were designed to function as new forms of participation and representation. They constitute the smallest representational units of the city and are supposed to channel and voice popular concerns and demands to the delegational and city authorities. Nevertheless, one recent case study of neighbourhood responses to insecurity has demonstrated that measures to establish closer and reliable relations between popular neighbourhoods and security agencies (for example, through launching a form of community policing) have not been very successful. It found low levels of popular participation and high levels of perceived insecurity (Alvarado et al. 2005).

The failure of popular activism to make a mark on the debate about insecurity stands in contrast to the influence of elite organizations on the policy agenda. One of Mexico's leading business associations, COPARMEX, was behind the project to consult Giuliani and financed it. COPARMEX was also very active in what, to date, has been the largest civic manifestation directed against insecurity in Mexico City. At the end of June 2004, powerful interest groups organized a silent march that attracted around 250,000 people. With massive support from the electronic media these organizations were able to stage a large-scale event that was, however, politicized from the beginning and was perceived as an attack on the city's authorities. The attorney general of the Federal District, in his turn, accused the organizers of creating an 'atmosphere of terror' in the city.[22]

Lynching Most people in Mexico City are probably so used to it that they hardly notice it any more: middle- and upper-class neighbourhoods have privatized public space by putting up iron gates and hiring guards from one of the many private security companies. Without showing personal identification a visitor is not allowed to enter the street or even an entire district. It is a direct product of the widespread feelings of fear of assaults, burglaries and kidnappings. Poor neighbourhoods also suffer from different forms of crime, but their inhabitants lack the means to protect themselves in this manner. It is here that the guards who seal off the richer *colonias* live. Confronted with robberies, the recent wave of *narcomenudeo* and the (perceived) inefficiency of law enforcement agencies, the inhabitants are increasingly tempted to take justice into their own hands. In Mexico City, this has only occasionally taken the form of vigilantism. Instead, it takes the form of mobs that seriously beat, injure and even kill suspected criminals. Mostly the perpetrators have not been prosecuted. In some cases a (petty) thief has been caught in flagrante by local residents and 'punished' with extreme violence. Between 2001 and 2004, twenty-four such cases of popular lynching were reported.

What appears striking about the recent history of lynching in Mexico City is that most of it takes place in the four southern, more 'rural' and relatively less densely populated delegations of Tláhuac, Xochimilco, Tlalpan and Milpa Alta, which constitute an area that has consistently had the lowest crime rates in the Federal District. No simple statistical correlation between crime and its violent repudiation by the local populace in the form of lynching can thus be warranted. It appears that specific social and cultural characteristics of these communities play a key role. Many of these communities are originally *pueblos* that have been absorbed by the expanding metropolis. Urbanization and migration towards these poor communities during recent decades have put previous social structures and cultural institutions under increasing pressure. The pressures of social exclusion are aggravated by the more recent penetration of criminal activities, such as *narcomenudeo*.[23] The combination of the vulnerabilities of social exclusion, marginalization and public insecurity can lead to what one observer called outbursts of 'social hatred' (Azaola 2005: 4).

The recent history of lynching in Mexico City came to a sad climax in November 2004, when two police officials of the Federal Preventive Police were nearly beaten to death and then burnt alive by an infuriated crowd in San Juan Ixtayopan, in the delegation of Tláhuac.[24] A third official barely survived. What made this lynching distinctive was that the atrocious events were transmitted live on national television, while the authorities were unable to drum up a sufficiently large force to disperse the crowd and rescue the endangered police officers. The beatings were even interrupted so that a journalist could interview one of the victims. The incident, which became known as the 'Tláhuac case', sent shock waves through the nation. The cruel killing of two police officers and subsequent statements by the authorities exposed many of the contradictions that afflict the management of Mexico City's problems of insecurity and violence.[25]

First, it became known that the federal police officers involved had been carrying out an undercover investigation in San Juan for weeks, but the local authorities had not been informed. The police officers had taken pictures and videos of the surroundings of a local school, thereby triggering rumours that they wanted to steal children. On that fatal 23 November, rumours surfaced that two children had actually been abducted, so local residents violently captured the officers. The Federal Preventive Police first declared that they were investigating kidnappings, but quickly changed their story and stated that they were involved in combating *narcomenudeo*. Later it was reported that they were after a leader of the violent guerrilla movement Ejército Popular Revolucionario (EPR), and hence that the carnage had been the result of conscious manipulation by EPR agents.[26] Whatever the real reasons for the presence of secret police in San Juan Ixtayopan, it became evident that the operation was not carried out in coordination with local police forces, who were then left with the task of resolving the situation. Even when the tragic events unfolded between six and nine o'clock that night the different Mexico City police forces were unable to launch a joint operation.[27] One local resident was adamant in his judgement: 'Nobody knew what they were doing, they didn't coordinate and lacked the resolve to act. What is the purpose of paying four million dollars to that stupid Giuliani?'[28]

Second, the Tláhuac case dramatically exemplified the huge gap in and crisis of trust between ordinary citizens and law enforcement agencies. People involved in the lynching knew perfectly well that their victims were police officers, but instead of this diminishing their suspicion about their activities it increased it. When a small group of local police officers and local authorities arrived at the scene, they were repelled by a mob which appeared to have grown with the arrival of a youth gang that incited the residents to lynch the victims. In a perceptive article, Azaola (2005: 9) has suggested that the events demonstrate the enormous distance that separates society from the police, but also that the police has many reasons for distancing itself from the population. The following day the police violently raided San Juan in search of the culprits, thereby adding more fuel to an already inflammable situation.

Third, the serious organizational, operational and technical shortcomings of the different law enforcement agencies in handling the situation were immediately politicized – that is, they became part of the intense political struggle between the political establishment of the Federal District and the federal government. Tláhuac thus underscores the fact that political rivalries and other conflicts of interest gravely undermine the willingness and decisiveness needed to reform and improve law enforcement and confront Mexico City's growing problems of insecurity and violence.

Conclusions

Mexico City is a bustling metropolis that houses all the contradictions of post-colonial societies. The tensions and contradictions resulting from the country's socio-economic structure have a long history in the metropolis, but in recent decades these have been exacerbated by the effects of neo-liberal economic and institutional reforms and recurring economic crises. Impoverishment, exclusion and inequality have created an urban landscape characterized by extreme differences in wealth and physical traits and a fragmentation of social space. All this is characteristically expressed in the emergence of gated neighbourhoods, apartment complexes and shopping malls, guarded by tens of thousands of badly paid private policemen, while poor and deprived working-class *colonias* persist in the central areas of the metropolis and, above all, in the densely populated zones at the ever widening periphery. This socio-economic panorama is further complicated by political shifts in the country which have had major repercussions in the capital. Throughout this chapter we have pointed to the consequences of the rivalries and open conflicts between different political players, parties and interest groups in and around Mexico City.

In addition, different forms of organized crime have taken firm roots in Mexico City. Particular areas in the city specialize in certain branches, such as arms dealing, contraband, automobile theft and stealing of car parts, kidnapping and, more recently, drug trafficking. There is ample evidence of the involvement of the different security forces.

While it has been observed that fear of crime and violence and the generalized perception of insecurity are relatively recent phenomena in Mexico City (Chevigny 2003: 89), the combined effects of increasing inequality and deepening exclusion, political transformations and organized crime have now put them firmly on the agenda of the authorities and the population at large. We have pointed out the connections between severe economic downturns and the rise of criminal offences and insecurity. The association between social and economic exclusion on the one hand and insecurity and violence on the other hand has, however, another side as well. While the demands for more penal justice and transparency should be seen as part of the claims for an extension of democracy and social justice, it is equally true that the fundamental social causes of much contemporary violence and crime are ruled out in the responses to the phenomenon. The social and political nature of crime and violence in Mexico City is increasingly obscured by discourses of policing and penal justice, the adoption of 'zero tolerance' being the clearest example. In this context it is important to note that insidious mob lynchings have been suggested as indications, albeit perverse, of powerful political claims for local autonomy and justice (Snodgrass Godoy 2004).

This is not to say that reform of the security forces and the justice system at large, as well as the struggle against impunity, merely deflect from the social agenda. We have drawn attention to the serious problems of coordination, rivalry, corruption and criminal behaviour that characterize Mexico City's security forces. This is unquestionably related to what we believe is a key feature of Mexico City's crime and insecurity governance system, namely its degree of politicization. The rivalries between different police forces and authorities, corruption, the events following the civic march against insecurity as well as the follow-up to the Tláhuac lynchings are all permeated by political agendas. This goes beyond confrontations between particular leaders and parties and is instead rooted in the systemic imbalances between executive, legislative and judicial powers and specific political cultural practices and traditions. The problems of violence and insecurity are, therefore, in the end problems of social justice and democracy.

Notes

We would like to thank Lizbeth Cruz of the Comisión de Seguridad Pública of the Asamblea Legislativa del Distrito Federal for her generous help during our research.

1 Fieldwork notes by Wil Pansters, April 2005.

2 Chevigny (2003) has argued that in the light of the growing limitations of the neo-liberal state in terms of distributing spoils, politicians are tempted to appeal to fear of violence and crime. See also Arteaga Botello (2004).

3 Other publications suggest that the number is much higher. Reames (2003: 4), for example, refers to more than 25 million.

4 For a recent and comprehensive overview of different aspects of life in Mexico City, see the hefty volume edited by Gustavo Garza (2000).

5 The most important municipalities in this ring are Ecatepec, Naucalpan and Tlalnepantla in the north and Nezahualcoyotl in the east, accounting for almost 4.5 million people.

6 Alvarado and Davis (2001) have formulated some tentative ideas about the relationships between recent political and institutional changes and the increase of violence and insecurity in Mexico. For political change and governance in the DF, see Alvarado and Davis (2003).

7 For a detailed historical study of crime in Mexico City in the first decades of the twentieth century, see Piccato (2001). For an early assessment of the geography of crime in Mexico City, see Hayner (1946).

8 The most important surveys were carried out by the newspaper *Reforma* (yearly since 1997), the Unidad de Análisis sobre Violencia Social of the UNAM and the Instituto Ciudadano de Estudios sobre la Inseguridad AC.

9 Gustavo Castillo García, 'La guerra entre cárteles, sin cuartel; 800 ejecutados en lo que va del año', in *La Jornada*, 7 August 2005, pp. 6–7.

10 Patricia Méndez, 'Preocupa a capitalinos narcomenudeo', *Reforma*, 18 May 2004.

11 See Raúl Monge, 'El atlas de la droga en el DF', *Proceso*, 27 March 2005, pp. 16–19.

12 Interview with JM, a former high-ranking Internal Affairs police officer, Mexico City, 11 April 2005; on the question of autonomy, see also Silva (2004).

13 Silva (2004) identified these patterns of police abuses on the basis of an analysis of the cases submitted to human rights organizations.

14 Interview with JL, Mexico City, 8 April 2005.

15 *Informe de Actividades correspondiente del 1 de enero de 2003 al 1 de enero del 2004*, of the Procuraduría General de Justicia del Distrito Federal, Archivo de la Comisión de Seguridad Pública de la Asamblea del Distrito Federal, Mexico City, p. 5.

16 Alejandro Gutiérrez, 'PFP: mafias intocables', *Proceso*, no. 1500, 31 July 2005, pp. 26–30. Another source mentioned that ordinary police officers have to pay around 40 dollars each month to preserve their jobs. See Arroyo (2003: 10).

17 See <www.inegi.gob.mx/est/librerias/tabulados.asp?tabulado=tab_p002a&c=706&e>.

18 Interview with JM. See also Alvarado and Davis (2001: 141), Mexico City, 11 April 2005.

19 Ibid.

20 Giuliani-SSP report, Mexico City, 7 August 2003, <www.ssp.df.gob.mx/htmls/ssp_sec_informe_giuliani_i.html>.

21 See, for example, Instituto de Seguridad y la Democracia to Marcelo Ebrard, Secretary of Public Security of the Federal District, 28 August 2003, <www.insydeideas.org>; Rob O. Varenik (2003), 'Los riesgos de la era Giuliani', <www.lchr.org>, consulted 13 April 2005; Arroyo (2003).

22 *La Jornada*, 25 June 2005.

23 *Reforma*, 12 December 2004.

24 See also Luis Hernández Navarro, 'San Juan Ixtayopan', *La Jornada*, 26 November 2004. In order to counteract problems of insecurity, the local government had taken initiatives earlier that year to increase the number of patrol cars and to introduce a neighbourhood police that would cooperate with the local population. See *La Jornada*, 6 June 2004, <www.jornada.unam.mx/2004/06/06/039n2cap.php?origen=capital.php&fly=1>.

25 The Tláhuac case has been reconstructed on the basis of newspaper reports and, more importantly, testimonies given by the authorities formally responsible for the case to a special investigation committee set up by the Asamblea Legislativa del DF. The authorities interrogated by the committee were Marcelo Ebrard, Secretary of Public Security of the Federal District, 6 December 2004; Regino García, Under-Secretary of Public Security of the Federal District, 5 January 2005; Fátima Mena Ortega, *delegada* of Tláhuac, 3 January 2005. The records of these interrogations are in the archives of the Comisión de Seguridad Pública of the Asamblea Legislativa del Distrito Federal in Mexico City.

26 For information about the relationship between Tláhuac and the EPR see Jorge Torres, 'Contrainteligencia guerrillera', *Proceso*, no. 1466, 5 December 2004, pp. 6–12.

27 Much of the detailed information about the lack of cooperation between different police forces and other aspects of the events can be found in the archives of the Asamblea Legislativa del Distrito Federal which formed the Comisión Especial para la Investigación de los Hechos Ocurridos en San Juan Ixtayopan and organized hearings with several authorities, such as the Secretary of Public Security and the chief of the Delegation of Tláhuac. The verbatim reports of these hearings contain detailed reconstructions of what happened that night and during its aftermath.

28 Arturo Cano, 'Linchamiento en Tláhuac. Del rumor a la barbarie', *La Jornada*, 28 November 2004.

4 | Medellín

RALPH ROZEMA*

For weeks camera crews dominated the small alleys of one of the working-class neighbourhoods in Medellín. Actress Flora Martínez, in her role as Rosario, a young attractive woman in her twenties, is the focus of the scene as she dances with the locals. Music reverberates through the vast neighbourhood built against the steep hills at the outskirts of this Colombian city of more than 2 million inhabitants. As the images roll on, the scene suddenly shows an outburst of violence, bringing the residents, who are taking part as natural actors, back to the 1980s and 1990s, when violence was part of daily life. The beautiful Rosario embodies the contradictions of Medellín of that time. When she dances seductively with her friends no one would think of her as one of the *sicarias* or hired killers responsible for the death of many residents in Medellín. The story of Rosario – based on the international bestseller *Rosario Tijeras* by Jorge Franco – is a story of tenderness in a city at war, which could probably have happened only in Medellín in these years of extreme violence (Franco 2004; Semana 2004).

The presence of an international film crew in one of the working-class neighbourhoods of Medellín, known for its violence, indicates a change. The infamous drugs cartel and its hired killers are history now. The recent demobilization of hundreds of right-wing paramilitaries has further improved the security situation in Medellín. And although armed groups are still present in the city, the level of violence has diminished significantly. At the end of 2004 the number of homicides reached its lowest point in thirty years (although still seventy-eight) (El Colombiano 2004); in May 2005 the number had further dropped to fifty-five. Critics, however, maintain that the peace process is fragile and that the reintegration of ex-combatants is still under way.

Armed groups have played a dominant role in working-class neighbourhoods of Colombian cities since the eighties. Over the years an incredible variety of armed groups have emerged: *bandas* (gangs), left-wing militias, *narcotraficantes* (drugs traffickers), *sicarios* (hired killers), *oficinas* (sophisticated criminal organizations), death squads dedicated to social cleansing, guerrilla fighters of the FARC, ELN and CAP, and various groups of right-wing paramilitaries. The armed actors formed intricate networks of power relations. While some groups confronted each other to gain control of strategic places, others stayed in the same territory, in some kind of hierarchical order. In Medellín armed groups sometimes occupied micro-areas the size of a street block (Pécaut 1999).

This chapter describes the history of urban violence in Medellín, the types of armed groups present, the daily life in neighbourhoods where armed groups such as guerrillas and paramilitaries make the rules, and the responses of the local government to the violence, including the recent peace initiative with paramilitaries.

A history of urban violence in Medellín

Medellín, the second city of Colombia, has expanded rapidly over the last decades, creating a patchwork of working-class neighbourhoods in the hills surrounding the city centre. Modern office buildings and shopping areas in the centre contrast with these neighbourhoods, where violence for so long dominated daily life. A modern and fast metropolitan train connects the two worlds. The population of Medellín has grown from 360,000 inhabitants in the early 1950s to around 2 million in 2005. Migrants moved to Medellín in search of economic opportunities; others came as refugees from the countryside owing to increasing violence between guerrillas and paramilitaries. Especially in the neighbourhoods in the north-east and the north-west, migrants arrived with few resources. But the invasion in the north-east (Nororiental) was more chaotic, resulting in small alleys meandering in all directions, while in the north-west (Noroccidental) the government intervened by planning some of the streets. But both working-class neighbourhoods still lack public places such as parks or plazas. In the 1980s El Poblado (south-east) turned into an elite neighbourhood where the new rich settled, among them those who made a fortune in the drugs trade (Jaramillo et al. 1998: 33; Daza 2001: 70). Despite the vibrant economic life in the city centre, the fierce international competition and the ongoing war have led to growing unemployment and poverty among the inhabitants, especially those living in the *comunas* on the outskirts of Medellín. Estimates suggest that by 2004 around 60 per cent of the urban population was living below the poverty line, while 50 per cent of all children were undernourished and did not attend school on a regular basis (Koonings and Leestemaker 2004: 140). At the beginning of 2005 the unemployment rate was around 15 per cent (ICER 2005). Industrial companies have been especially reluctant to employ people from working-class neighbourhoods known for their confrontations between armed groups.

When looking closer at Medellín's history it becomes clear that the city has not always been in the grip of violence. In the 1960s and 1970s Medellín was known as a prosperous industrial city pleasantly located in the green hills of the department of Antioquia. The crime rate was low, and a single murder would appear on the newspapers' front pages. The tranquillity of the city changed in the 1980s with the advent of the Medellín drugs cartel. Residents argue that Pablo Escobar, leader of the infamous cartel, has strongly influenced the mentality of the Paisas, as the inhabitants of Medellín are known. Young people, who previously would have done anything to get a decent job, now go for the quick money of organized crime. Escobar founded a private army of hundreds of *sicarios* or mercenaries, who assassinated members of competing drug gangs as well as politicians, officials and businessmen who refused to cooperate with the cartel.

The death of Escobar in 1992 preceded the fall of the Medellín drugs cartel. A substantial part of the drugs trade was taken over by cartels in other parts of the country (principally the Cali cartel), but the level of violence in Medellín did not diminish. Many *sicarios* of the former Medellín cartel, who had lost their jobs, decided to take part in or form new criminal (youth) gangs that ravaged the city for years. The expansion of these criminal gangs provoked a reaction, especially in the Nororiente (north-east), where popular militia were formed. These illegal *milicias* adopted political views close to those of left-wing guerrillas elsewhere in Colombia and were formed to protect the civil population of the Nororiente against the ravages of criminal gangs. The many armed confrontations did not, however, make the neighbourhoods safer. In 1994 negotiations between the government and the *milicias* finally led to their demobilization. Some of the former *milicias* took part in a new security service, Coosercom, which patrolled the same neighbourhoods. A few years later, however, Coosercom was dissolved when it became clear that members had abused their power among the civil population.

In the period 1995–2000 negotiations between different youth gangs were actively supported by the Roman Catholic Church and by the local government. The high crime rate in the neighbourhoods was mainly due to the youth gangs, and hundreds of teenagers had already lost their lives in armed confrontations between different gangs. Around sixty gangs in the north-east, the east and north-west of the city came to a peace agreement. Although in the first months after the agreements many young people's lives were saved, it became clear that in the long run the number of deaths did not diminish. New gangs were formed, while some neighbourhoods were terrorized by gangs that had succeeded in getting a monopoly, as was the case with La Terraza and Frank in different parts of the Nororiente. Finally the municipality of Medellín decided to suspend the negotiation process with the gangs.

In the same period guerrilla movements such as the FARC and ELN invaded the neighbourhoods at the outskirts of the city and established their own regimes, especially in Comuna 13 in the western hills of Medellín. These invasions were in line with the new policies of the guerrilla movements to establish bases in the city and to control strategic exit points to the north and east of the country. In the wake of the guerrilla movements right-wing paramilitaries entered the city (Balbín 2004; IPC 2003; Jaramillo et al. 1998; Villa Martínez et al. 2003).

The illegal paramilitary groups in Colombia originated in small private vigilante groups formed by landowners to defend their property against the guerrillas. These groups, which initially operated only in the countryside, formed a national organization, Autodefensas Unidas de Colombia (AUC). The ideology of the paramilitaries is to establish law and order. They fight the guerrillas but often also eliminate those suspected of supporting the guerrillas, a tactic that has resulted in widespread massacres, assassinations and human rights violations.

In Medellín armed confrontations between paramilitaries and the guerrillas have claimed many casualties, especially among the civilian population. The guerrillas were finally ousted by the paramilitaries. In the case of Comuna 13 it was the army which defeated the guerrilla groups. Between 1998 and 2000 paramilitaries dominated most of the working-class neighbourhoods in Medellín, and they took control of the youth gangs. It is generally understood that although the paramilitaries oppressed the local population by imposing their own order, violence by youth gangs diminished when they came under the control of the paramilitaries. In some cases paramilitaries incorporated members of the youth gangs. In 2004 heavy armed confrontations occurred between different factions of paramilitaries. The Bloque Cacique Nutibara (BCN) finally expelled the Bloque Metro from Medellín and incorporated some of its fighters. From then on BCN controlled around 70 per cent of the city (Balbín 2004; Salazar 1994; Vélez Rendón 2001; Villa Martínez et al. 2003; Noche y Niebla 2003; El Mundo Magazine 2003).

Daily life under guerrillas and paramilitaries

Describing the intricate mosaic of armed actors and its often arbitrary violence, Pécaut (1999) introduced the notion of the 'banality of violence'. With the proliferation of various types of armed groups, violence had become 'routinized' and 'normalized' as an essential part of the functioning of

Colombian society. Moser and McIlwaine (1999) proposed dividing violence into three categories: *political violence* to obtain political power (guerrilla and paramilitary activities); *economic violence* to obtain economic power (drugs trafficking and street crime); and *social violence* (domestic violence). The effects of violence may also be categorized. While accurate measurements of *direct costs* (loss of life, disability and loss of property) are essential, they are not sufficient to derive an overall view that includes the erosion of social, human and physical capital. *Erosion of social capital* means the loss of trust and cooperation within formal and informal organizations, the loss of social structures. Violence also leads to the *erosion of human capital*: the deterioration of the health and nutrition of individuals and the loss of investment in education and healthcare. *Erosion of physical capital* manifests itself in the form of loss of investment in infrastructure and the business sector, and the loss of employment (Moser and McIlawaine 1999).

In Medellín the loss of life reached its highest point in the 1980s. The most dangerous were neighbourhoods disputed by guerrillas and paramilitaries where armed confrontations were part of daily life (Restrepo 2004: 175). Loss of social structures was evident when fighting in a neighbourhood continued over an extended period. When the local conflict increased, more and more residents left for a quieter place elsewhere in the city. But those with no relatives elsewhere or with few resources had no other option than to stay. Gloria Posada lived in 2002 on the verge of Comuna 13 when guerrillas and paramilitaries had armed confrontations in her block: 'Around us more and more lights of neighbouring houses disappeared. Tension increased day by day. For us coming home had become like a survival trip every day. Silence had replaced the usual liveliness in the streets, while suddenly loud explosions could be heard near by or further away in the hills. [...] We found the rhythm of the confrontations outside reflected in our breathing and in the beating of our heart' (El Tiempo 2003).

When only a guerrilla movement or a paramilitary group is present in a neighbourhood violence is less frequent, but the residents often face repression by such an armed group, which imposes its own laws and order. This was especially the case in Comuna 13, which for a long time was dominated by guerrilla groups. Later the army expelled the guerrillas and then paramilitaries settled in Comuna 13, imposing their order on the residents. Although many residents emphasize the similarities between the regimes of the guerrillas and the paramilitaries there are important differences. Comuna 13 had fallen into the hands of different guerrilla movements: the FARC (Fuerzas Armados Revolucionarios de Colombia), the ELN (Ejército de Liberación Nacional) and the CAP (Comandos Armados del Pueblo, a breakaway section of the ELN). They all imposed their rules upon the civil population. But initially they tried to be friendly to the inhabitants. In the beginning residents did not have a problem with the guerrilla regime, as Manuel Ramirez, a twenty-five-year-old resident of Comuna 13, recounts. 'Initially the guerrillas had a positive influence. The movement imposed a kind of order, they prevented robberies, because they said it would be a bad example for the children. They organized cultural events with music, dance and video concerts. We liked it, the first months were all right' (Interview, April 2004).

After some time the guerrillas changed their attitude and started to use indiscriminate violence against the population. The most threatening aspect was that guerrilla fighters began to murder residents with opposing political ideas. 'They oppressed the population, they accused people and threatened them with arms. Those who refused to cooperate were assassinated,' said Manuel Ramirez. In Comuna 13 several guerrilla factions were disputing territory. Most respondents affirmed that the ELN (and its breakaway section, CAP) were more humane than the FARC, which often used arbitrary violence. All armed groups imposed their own laws upon the local population, but the FARC applied stricter rules than the other guerrilla groups, including a curfew, a prohibition on bringing visitors from the outside into the neighbourhood and 'revolutionary taxes' for shops and drivers of collective taxis. Moreover guerrilla leaders acted as judges. Sentences imposed by the FARC varied from cleaning the streets to capital punishment in case of robbery.

The armed groups tried to establish roots in the neighbourhood by recruiting new fighters locally. Both the guerrillas and the paramilitaries used this practice to strengthen their ranks. As job opportunities were low in the working-class neighbourhoods, teenagers felt attracted by the urban armed groups. One of them was Chila, a young *guerrillera* in her early twenties, whom I met shortly after she had deserted from the CAP in her neighbourhood, Comuna 13. She had decided to join the armed group after one of her friends convinced her to take part in its activities.

> In the early evening we had classes in a small group on ideology: Lenin and Che Guevara. At night we had our combat training, we worked with pistols and other weapons, everything was real from the start. I attended the training secretly, even my parents did not know about it. It was exciting, but at the same time I was afraid because one day the paramilitaries could find out about me and then murder my parents. It was an adventure, but with a huge risk. (Interview, April 2004)

The beginning of the guerrilla regime contrasts sharply with the arrival of the paramilitaries in Comuna 13 a few years later (this happened after the guerrillas were expelled by the national army). From the beginning the para-militaries were intimidating the local population and keeping their distance. Roberto Giraldo, a local resident, recounts how at the end of 2002 the para-militaries arrived.

> When the army had withdrawn its troops, other armed men took to the streets. At first we did not know who they were, then it turned out they were paramilitaries. They drove around in luxurious cars and expensive motor-bikes. In our neighbourhood we are not used to seeing such wealth. They took possession of the empty houses at the top of the hill. Later they moved into the neighbourhood, they sometimes bought or rented houses, but they also forced residents to leave their homes. They were patrolling the streets and intimidating the residents with their weapons. (Interview, April 2004)

The paramilitaries acted differently in the sense that people were not shot openly, but they let people whom they suspected of leftist political ideas disappear. Shortly after the arrival of the paramilitaries in Comuna 13 the first *desaparecidos* were reported. 'We received anonymous calls,' said Elisabeth Yarce, editor of Medellín's daily newspaper *El Colombiano*. 'People panicked when they found out that family members had disappeared. We could not believe it at first, but it turned out to be true.' Nelly Arango, who lives in the central part of Comuna 13, characterizes the differences between the guer-rillas and the paramilitaries. 'In this *barrio*, with the paramilitaries, reigns the law of silence. We were better off with the guerrillas, because they acted openly. You could get lost in a shooting, but at least you knew where the bullets were coming from. With the paramilitaries everything happens in secret. We do not know exactly who is responsible for the disappearances' (interview, April 2004).

Like the guerrillas, the paramilitaries introduced their own rules to control daily life in the neighbourhood. Most respondents agreed that differences between their rules and the guerrillas' were small, and in this respect they would not call either one better. Paramilitaries prohibited informal gather-ings in the streets. And like the guerrillas the paramilitaries collected taxes (*vacuna*) from shops, supermarkets and bus and taxi companies. When the paramilitaries had taken control of Comuna 13, they announced 400 vacan-cies. Teenagers felt attracted by opportunities for both money and status, but they knew that they would have to take part in armed operations in which they might risk their lives. Families came under severe strain when their sons enlisted in the paramilitary organization. 'One of my neighbours, a fourteen-year-old boy, decided to join the paramilitaries. His parents were in tears when they heard about it,' said Roberto Giraldo, exemplifying the drama many families had gone through.

Residents of the working-class neighbourhoods of Medellín have found their own responses to cope with armed groups. The continuing threat of violence means that residents impose restrictions in time and place on themselves. Moreover, fear produces shock waves that are more far reaching than the violence itself, anticipating and magnifying the death and the suffering. Calls for defensive reactions to imminent threat occasionally reach hysterical proportions (Restrepo 2004: 179). When we consider Restrepo's concept of the fragmentation of space, it becomes clear that fear of violence has resulted in the curtailment of many social spaces. Residents select streets and zones in which they can travel without danger. But with the increasing threat of violence transport becomes more and more limited. For years taxi drivers in Medellín avoided working-class neighbourhoods that were known for armed confrontations, such as the Nororiental, Noroccidental and Comuna 13. After the expulsion of the guerrillas, when the heavy fighting came to an end, most taxi drivers in Medellín resumed work in these neighbourhoods.

Violence and fear lead not only to restrictions in place, but also to restrictions in time. They shorten the future perspectives of individuals and communities as a whole. In the 1980s and 1990s the death toll in Medellín was so high that few residents had not lost a relative, neighbour or friend. In such an environment it is difficult to imagine a bright future, especially if you feel that you may face a similar fate yourself. In working-class neighbourhoods people tend not to make plans for the immediate future, let alone for a lifetime. This attitude has economic consequences as residents are hesitant to start their own businesses or invest money (Villa Martínez et al. 2003; Restrepo 2004: 181).

The mass media in Colombia play a reinforcing role in this respect, reproducing violent events in television shows and news bulletins. Restrepo (2004: 181) states that such an 'obsessive reiteration of tragedies sinks into the national memory, dimming future horizons. [...] Life is lived from day to day, and the home tends to turn into a transitory refuge.' But that is only one side of the media. The publicity departments of industrial companies tend to offer a positive and tantalizing perspective in their advertisements to neutralize uncertainty about the future, or, in the words of Villa Martínez et al. (2003: 183), to create a *comunidad imaginada*, an imagined community. While in violent neighbourhoods a menacing silence may paralyse social life, telecom company Orbitel promotes itself with the slogan: 'No more minutes of silence. Speak. Colombia will be the way you like it' (*No más minutos de silencio. Hable. Así Colombia será como usted quiere que sea*; ibid.: 183). The national organization of employers, ANDI, states that a spirit of optimism will renew confidence in peace and development. While ANDI refers to an entrepreneurial tradition that has boosted industry in Medellín since the nineteenth century, Villa Martínez goes a step farther, referring to the local culture of the Paisas, who have lived now for centuries in Medellín. Paisas, proud as they are, have so far withstood the civil war and will certainly find a solution. To be a Paisa is a guarantee of a future in times of uncertainty (ibid.: 185).

A more subtle way of escaping the daily threats relies on the cultural traditions of Colombia, conveying emotions through music and dance. It reveals a striking contradiction that exists in Medellín between, on the one hand, the atrocities of the violence and, on the other, the *alegría* (happiness) and celebrations, dancing while the bullets are whizzing around. This image of Medellín, as it emerged in the 1990s, inspired the imagination of writers and artists, most famous among them probably Jorge Franco, whose novel *Rosario Tijeras* is now a movie.

A promising peace process with the paramilitaries

The situation in Medellín is changing now, owing mainly to a process of negotiation with the paramilitaries which started in 2002 when the para-military organization AUC announced a unilateral truce. The truce and the subsequent negotiations were motivated by the desire of the paramilitaries to avoid extradition to the United States for drugs trafficking and to avoid long prison sentences in Colombia for massacres and human rights violations. Some observers argue that paramilitary leaders wanted to use a demobiliza-tion process as an opportunity to launder their money, obtained through the illicit drugs trade (Human Rights Watch 2005).

In 2003 President Álvaro Uribe authorized the then mayor of Medellín, Luis Pérez, to start an unprecedented experiment by coming to an accord with the local paramilitary group Bloque Cacique Nutibara (BCN). It was the first time ever in Colombia that such an accord was reached with a paramilitary group. National legislation to regulate such a mobilization did not exist at the time; parliamentary discussion of the Ley de Justicia y Paz (the law on justice and peace that would set sentences for demobilized paramilitaries accused of violating human rights) was yet to happen. A pre-condition for the project in Medellín was therefore that the demobilized paramilitaries had not been involved in human rights violations. For this reason a relatively new branch of the national paramilitary organization AUC was chosen: the BCN, only recently formed, but with a heavy presence in the working-class neighbourhoods of Medellín. On 25 November 2003, just before the end of Mayor Pérez's term of office, a ceremony took place in which 874 paramilitary fighters laid down their weapons. In the convention centre rows of men sang the national anthem and then handed over their AK-47s, old rifles and revolvers, although fewer than two hundred weapons in all (New York Times 2003; *Washington Post*, 25 November 2003; OAS 2005).

Disarmament is the first step in a process often described as DDRR (disarmament, demobilization, reinsertion and reintegration). In practice *disarmament* seldom means that all weapons are handed over, but even by surrendering some of their weapons the concerned group demonstrates its commitment to the peace process. The second step, *demobilization*, includes dismantling the structure of the military organization. *Reinsertion*, the transition from military to social life, entails a short period during which former combatants often feel vulnerable and have problems earning an income. If such problems persist, they may fall back on their former life as combatants. *Reintegration* is a process that takes more time and leads to the full participation of the demobilized combatants in social, economic and political activities in their neighbourhoods (Knight and Özerdem 2004).

The city government of Medellín developed an extensive programme for the demobilized paramilitaries: the Peace and Reconciliation Programme 'Return to Legality' (*Programa Paz y Reconciliación 'Regreso a la Legalidad'*). This programme included education, psycho-social counselling and courses on income generation. Some of the demobilized paramilitaries attended training courses for car mechanics, construction workers, cooks or salesmen. Others studied at universities or schools. And a few worked as interns in companies or institutions such as the general hospital, the local public television station Telemedellín, private security companies or car dealers. Six months after the demobilization ceremony 762 of the 874 demobilized paramilitaries had a paid job (*El Colombiano*, 23 May 2004). Most of the demobilized paramilitaries settled in their own neighbourhoods. A survey indicates that a majority of the residents feel positive about the presence in their neighbourhood of beneficiaries of the programme. In August 2004 76 per cent were positive about their presence; by January 2005 the percentage had increased to 88 per cent. But residents also expressed their doubts. In January 2005 41 per cent of the residents (this was 46 per cent in August 2004) believed that some of the beneficiaries of the programme would fall back into illegal activities and some affirmed that various demobilized paramilitaries had already been involved in illegal activities (Programa de Paz y de Reconciliación 2005). The peace accord aimed at full reintegration into society of the demobilized paramilitaries. This included possible membership of social and political organizations, such as neighbourhood committees and youth groups. Tensions arose especially when demobilized paramilitaries wanted to participate in the meetings of neighbourhood committees. But six months after the demobilization, during the local elections of 25 April 2004, various demobilized paramilitaries were elected to local boards, the Juntas de Acción Comunal de Medellín (JAC).

Nearly two years after the demobilization of the 874 paramilitaries in Medellín it is estimated that their reintegration has been completed successfully. The weekly *Semana* (2005) attributes this principally to the allocation of municipal funds for training and jobs. The most remarkable achievement, however, was the spectacular reduction in violence. In January 2001 the number of homicides was 310; in May 2005 it had fallen to fifty-five (Programa de Paz y de Reconciliación 2005).

In the course of the peace process, however, new problems also arose. In the beginning demobilized paramilitaries feared retaliation by other armed groups and complained about the security situation in their neighbourhoods. In the first year five demobilized paramilitaries were killed, and for some time a number of them did not live in their own neighbourhoods. At the time of the demobilization of the 874 BCN paramilitaries, paramilitaries from other factions of the umbrella organization AUC entered the working-class neighbourhoods of Medellín. This move undermined the local peace accord in which national representatives of the AUC had taken part. The new fighters, who took over the positions of the demobilized BCN, were paramilitaries from many different factions, such as the Bloque Elmer Cardenas, Héroes de Granada, Bloque José Luis Zuluaga and Héroes del Nordeste. These paramilitaries started to rule the neighbourhoods in much the same way as the now demobilized BCN (Balbín 2004). One difference between the new and the old paramilitaries was, however, that the new fighters maintained a low profile in the neighbourhoods; they did not show themselves so much, at least during the daytime, and the level of violence diminished. The presence of the new paramilitaries meant, however, that the local government and the police force were still not able to control these neighbourhoods, and that residents were once again subjected to their arbitrary rules. In the course of time some groups from among these new paramilitaries took part in other demobilizations.

Another problem was the increased activity of youth gangs. The para-militaries of the BCN had restricted the activities of the gangs in their own neighbourhoods, resulting in a lower level of common crime. With the de-mobilization of the BCN, however, the gangs took their chance, enhancing the crime rate in the working-class neighbourhoods. In some cases the gangs were incorporated in new paramilitary groups that had entered the neighbour-hood (ibid.).

Critics say that the spectacular reduction in violence is a result not only of the new municipal policy but also of paramilitary decisions. In this a key role is played by one of the most influential paramilitary leaders, Adolfo Paz, or Don Berna (officially Diego Fernando Murillo Bejerano), known as 'the pacificator of Medellín', who used his power to restrain the paramilitaries in Medellín, but at the same time directed a professional criminal organization known as La Oficina (Semana 2005). Paz, who was previously in the Medellín drugs cartel, had become famous by solving disputes between armed groups and thus saving many lives. His popularity gained in strength during the BCN demobilization process. But that is only one side of Adolfo Paz. Intel-ligence reports cited by *Semana* (ibid.) say that despite the demobilization process Paz did not dismantle the military structure of his paramilitary group and that he continues to head the criminal organization La Oficina. Accord-ing to these sources La Oficina is comparable to the former network of the hired killers of Pablo Escobar, but with more resources, more sophisticated technology and tentacles in various businesses. In May 2005 Don Berna was arrested in connection with the murder of a local politician in Córdoba; it is not yet clear whether new leaders have taken over his role, or whether this has changed the attitude of the paramilitaries in Medellín. Critics have expressed concern that the reduction of violence in Medellín is partly due to the influence of paramilitary leaders; it is not the legitimate state which takes care of the security of its citizens, but instead a sort of parallel 'state' that weakens the democratic institutions (ibid.). Social scientist Jesús Balbin comes to a similar conclusion: 'Despite the improvements we are worried because there are zones of the city in the hands of illegal armed groups and also in these zones the number of murders and robberies has fallen, but the control is not in the hands of the state. There is a feeling of security in some neighbourhoods, but it is not a security based on democratic citizenship' (El Colombiano, 2004).

In the longer term the government of Medellín is focusing on social de-velopment in the working-class neighbourhoods. The idea is to discourage people from participating in armed groups through education and economic incentives. The programme includes credits for starting enterprises and business courses for youths. The national organization of employers, ANDI, contributes to the programme. ANDI has been one of the prominent actors within civil society supporting a peace process on the basis of negotiations (Koonings and Leestemaker 2004: 142). To improve living conditions in the densely built working-class neighbourhoods the city government wants to create public spaces such as parks and plazas. 'With the diminishing violence residents do not need to restrict themselves to their private places, they can go out. We want to create an open atmosphere with squares and parks to give life back to the neighbourhoods,' as one government official said.

Concluding remarks

The seemingly endless neighbourhoods covering the hills around Medellín's city centre are experiencing a process of rapid change. For years armed groups ravaged the neighbourhoods, but unlike in cities such as Rio de Janeiro the situation in Medellín has been much more volatile, often with new armed actors moving in, forming intricate webs of power relations. Armed groups established oppressive regimes in the working-class neighbourhoods, preventing government institutions from fulfilling their legal role (Restrepo 2004; Villa Martínez et al. 2003). As a result of the rapidly changing pattern among the armed groups, even residents of the neighbourhoods often did not know exactly which leader of which armed group was in power. The working-class neighbourhoods of Medellín reflect the findings of Pécaut (1999) about a situation in which the use of violence becomes routine. Fear among the residents has resulted in the erosion of social capital, as referred to by Moser (2004) and Concha-Eastman (2002), affecting the trust and social relationships of the residents. Recently the city government of Medellín has initiated a peace process with paramilitaries which so far has resulted in the demobilization of 874 combatants. Although the process of reintegrating the demobilized paramilitaries is still under way, violence has been reduced dramatically, to its lowest level in thirty years. Critics maintain, however, that new paramilitaries from other regions have entered the working-class neighbourhoods and, although they are keeping a low profile, their presence may still be a threat to the fragile peace process. Looking back, it is remarkable that even at the height of the conflict residents found ways to survive. One of the most striking contradictions in Medellín is the contrast between the atrocities of the armed conflict and celebrations in the form of music and dance. For outsiders it may be difficult to imagine Rosario dancing while elsewhere in the neighbourhood the bullets are whizzing around. Residents emphasize the importance of celebrations not only as a natural aspect of Colombian society, but also as way to survive a situation of war.

Note

* The research on which this chapter is based has been partly funded by a travel grant from the Netherlands' Foundation for the Advancement of Tropical Research (NWO/WOTRO).

5 | Managua

DENNIS RODGERS

This chapter explores the emergence of new forms of urban segregation in contemporary Managua, Nicaragua. Although the country has historically always been characterized by high levels of socio-economic inequality – with the notable exception of the Sandinista revolutionary period (1979–90), when disparities declined markedly – the past decade in particular has seen the development of new processes of exclusion and differentiation, especially in urban areas. In many ways, these are part of a broader regional trend; as several recent studies – including the other chapters of this volume – have noted, many other Latin American cities are undergoing similar mutations. The seminal investigation in this regard is undoubtedly Caldeira's *City of Walls* (2000), which traces the way in which rising crime and insecurity have changed the cityscape of São Paulo, Brazil, transforming it from a space of open circulation to a fragmented archipelago of isolated 'fortified en-claves'. This new urban morphology is most visible in the proliferation of self-sufficient gated communities and closed condominiums for the affluent, which have significantly altered the character of urban space as those on the 'inside' of the enclaves no longer relate to notions of spatial cohabitation with those on the 'outside', but rather to an ideal of separation from them.[1]

In urban Nicaragua, the phenomenon has arguably gone farther than simply enclaves. As I have detailed elsewhere (Rodgers 2004a), urban segrega-tion has in fact developed through a process of 'disembedding' rather than fragmentation. Partly because of the small size of the Managua elite, what has emerged instead of gated communities and closed condominiums is a 'fortified network', which has been constituted through the selective and purposeful construction of high-speed roads connecting the spaces of the elites within the city: their homes, offices, clubs, bars, restaurants, shop-ping malls and the international airport. The poor are excluded from these locations by private security, but also from the connecting roads, which are cruised at breakneck speeds by expensive 4x4 cars, and have no traffic lights but only roundabouts, meaning that those in cars avoid having to stop – and risk being carjacked – but those on foot risk their lives when they try to cross a road. The general picture, in other words, is one whereby a whole 'layer' of Managua's urban fabric has been 'ripped out' of the metropolis for the exclusive use of the city elites, thereby profoundly altering the cityscape and the relations between social groups within it.

Such processes of segregation and exclusion are largely being driven by the affluent urban elites, both in Nicaragua and elsewhere in Latin America. This is obvious in the nature of the urban transformations themselves, but also becomes apparent when one 'follow[s] the money', as the Watergate mole 'Deep Throat' – aka Mark Felt – famously advised. Managua's transformation coincided with the accession to power of Arnoldo Alemán, whose presidency between 1997 and 2001 came to epitomize the new oligarchy that emerged in Nicaragua from the ruins of the Sandinista revolution and the post-conflict peace process (see Rocha 2002), and at whose benefit the city's mutations are clearly directed. The vast majority of the infrastructural changes to Managua's cityscape were in fact financed by the Office of the Presidency – rather than the Managua municipality, which actually saw its budget significantly reduced – and were moreover among the few of Alemán's actions that were uncontested by the Sandinista opposition, the upper ranks of which have themselves become part of the new oligarchy. Overall, several hundreds of millions of US dollars were spent on what can arguably be said to have constituted an orchestrated top-down process of urban transformation primarily to the advantage of the city elites and not the impoverished majority of the city population.

While it is clearly critically important to consider this top-down perspective, it also arguably constitutes something of a case of 'elite-centrism'. I use the term 'elite-centrism' not because I think that contemporary analyses of urban segregation in Latin American cities favour elites – few of them do – but rather to point to the fact that such processes are generally always seen as flowing 'from above', and are almost exclusively explored in relation to the fortified enclaves or networks of the elites. These, however, have an inevitable flipside in the form of concomitant 'zones of exclusion', where the vast majority of the excluded live and frequently eke out a living on limited resources. The dynamics of this 'planet of slums' – to use Davis's (2004) evocative expression – are just as worthy of consideration, as they are characterized by bottom-up processes that are also leading to critical urban mutations, including in particular the development of forms of what might be labelled 'urban segregation from below'. This chapter presents a case study of such processes in a poor Managua neighbourhood called Barrio Luis Fanor Hernández,[2] drawing on ethnographic field research carried out in 1996/97 and 2002/03.[3] In particular, it explores how the emergence of a local drugs economy in the late 1990s led to a process of profound socio-economic differentiation in the neighbourhood, fostering a range of different types of cultural and material exclusions. The chapter describes these in detail and relates them to wider structural factors and processes, including a political economy of Nicaragua's general economic predicament.

Barrio Luis Fanor Hernández: past and present

Barrio Luis Fanor Hernández is a low-income neighbourhood located in south-east Managua. It was founded in the early 1960s by squatters on what was then fallow farmland on the outskirts of Managua, and rapidly became informally known as *La Sobrevivencia*, due to the fact that it was reputedly one of the poorest neighbourhoods in the city where 'people were always hungry and nobody did anything other than survive', according to a long-time resident called Don Manuel. Following the Sandinista revolution in 1979, the neighbourhood benefited from the new regime's urban reconstruction programme and was completely rebuilt in 1980/81. Under the supervision of government personnel, and with materials donated by the Cuban government, local inhabitants collectively built basic housing for themselves, as well as roads, paths, drains and public spaces.[4] This reconstruction programme called for follow-up maintenance by the state, however, and this never materialized, partly because public resources became increasingly diverted towards financing the costly civil war that affected the country from the mid-1980s onwards. The neighbourhood infrastructure rapidly began to decay, and by the time I first visited Barrio Luis Fanor Hernández in 1996, the majority of houses were falling apart, and the neighbourhood infrastructure was deteriorating badly. Public spaces had been converted into rubbish dumps, cracks and potholes blemished roads and paths, and drains were blocked and no longer working.[5]

This infrastructural decay was mirrored socio-economically. Although the neighbourhood was never well off by any stretch of the imagination during the 1980s, even after being reconstructed, the revolutionary regime ensured that at the very least nobody went hungry, through the general distribution of basic food rations to poor households. Following regime change in 1990, many *barrio* inhabitants felt that their living conditions declined, and indeed, by the mid-1990s the situation had become so bad that many residents were saying: 'We've come full circle back to the time of *La Sobrevivencia*.' Certainly, according to a survey that I carried out in Barrio Luis Fanor Hernández in November 1996, the neighbourhood unemployment rate was over 45 per cent, with a further 25 per cent of those economically active underemployed.[6] There was little local economic enterprise in the neighbourhood apart from theft and delinquency, and there were moreover few opportunities outside the *barrio* either, especially for a labour force that tended to be unskilled. Most of those who worked did so in the informal sector, and the median monthly income was around 700 córdobas (about US$85 at the time) – although many earned less. Not surprisingly, perhaps, the strains on the social fabric were such that it was no exaggeration to talk about a veritable 'atomization' of social life (see also Nitlapán-*Envío* team 1995; Núñez 1996). In spite of this social fragmentation, however, there was nevertheless a certain socio-economic uniformity to the *barrio*, with very few individuals or households being visibly better off than the rest.

I expected little to have changed when I returned to Barrio Luis Fanor Hernández in 2002 – considering that Nicaragua's macroeconomic situation had not improved – and it therefore came as a great surprise when one of the first things I observed on entering the neighbourhood was clear signs of significant economic improvement. Most obviously, much of what had been a relatively uniform neighbourhood of ramshackle, mainly wooden houses had been very visibly ameliorated, with many houses now made of brick and concrete, as well as having been expanded. Moreover, I counted over a dozen cars in the *barrio* streets as I walked into the neighbourhood – and subsequently recorded that there were a total of seventy-two cars in the *barrio* – most of which evidently belonged to the households in front of which they were parked. This was in striking contrast to five years previously, when there had been just five car-owners in the neighbourhood. Finally, as I greeted old friends and acquaintances, it was immediately obvious that a significant number were dressed in better-quality clothes than before, many wore ostentatious gold jewellery and designer sunglasses, and some even had mobile telephones (and this in a neighbourhood where only a dozen households had had land lines in the mid-1990s).

Although this was not what I had come to research – I had returned primarily to conduct a follow-up study to my previous investigations on gang violence in the neighbourhood (Rodgers 2000) – I straight away set about trying to find out what was fuelling this process of economic improvement. One immediately obvious fact was that the betterment was not universal. Many houses in the neighbourhood remained unchanged compared to five years previously, and moreover neither roads nor drains had been improved, public spaces continued to be rubbish dumps, and public lighting was still non-existent. As such, the source of the economic improvement was likely private rather than public. It was also a process that seemed to affect different parts of Barrio Luis Fanor Hernández differently – there seemed to be more economic improvement in the '*arriba*' (western) side of the neighbour-hood than in the '*abajo*' (eastern) side – and moreover differently compared to surrounding neighbourhoods. Although there were signs of economic improvements in all of these, they were occurring on a lesser scale. This was particularly obvious from the perspective of housing: almost 60 per cent of houses in Barrio Luis Fanor Hernández had improved compared to the mid-1990s, but in surrounding neighbourhoods only about 20 per cent bore any signs of major upgrading.

Drugs, material wealth and conspicuous consumption

It quickly became apparent that there were actually three distinct processes contributing to the economic development and concomitant socio-economic differentiation visible in Barrio Luis Fanor Hernández and surrounding neighbourhoods. Two of these seemed common to all, namely the increased sending of remittances by migrants abroad and the spread of credit facilities which allowed many with low incomes to buy cars and become taxi-owners (see Rodgers 2004b). The third was drug trafficking, and this occurred in a particular way in Barrio Luis Fanor Hernández, to the extent that there is little doubt that it constituted the key factor for the almost 40 per cent difference in its infrastructural enhancement compared to surrounding neighbourhoods. Although there was some drug dealing in the neighbourhoods around Barrio Luis Fanor Hernández, this happened on a very small scale. Indeed, the small-time drug dealers that operated in surrounding neighbourhoods would generally come and buy their wares in Barrio Luis Fanor Hernández, which by all accounts had become one of Managua's principal drug distributing neighbourhoods, where drugs were brought in from outside the city and from where they were disseminated within.

Drug dealing was by no means new to Barrio Luis Fanor Hernández. In the mid-1990s, marijuana had been sold in the neighbourhood, albeit only on a small scale by two individuals who grew it themselves. Their main clients had been the local youth gang. By 2002, however, this artisanal trade had been completely superseded by a cocaine-based drug economy which principally involved the sale of crack, better known in Nicaragua as '*la piedra*', or 'the stone'.[7] To a large extent this transformation is linked to broader international factors. Owing to improved law enforcement efforts in the Caribbean, the late 1990s saw a diversification of drug trafficking routes from Colombia to North America, with flows along the Mexican–Central American corridor increasing dramatically. Due to its proximity to the Colombian Caribbean island of San Andrés, Nicaragua is geographically a natural trans-shipment point along this route, but had previously been under-exploited because its transport infrastructure was generally very poor and traffic through the country was slight, making it difficult to slip drug shipments through unnoticed. In late 1998, however, Nicaragua was devastated by Hurricane Mitch, suffering major infrastructure damage and resource drainage. This negatively affected the already limited capabilities of local law enforcement organizations, thereby facilitating the importation of drugs. Furthermore, post-Mitch reconstruction efforts focused largely on rebuilding transport links, and improved these substantially, which had the knock-on effect of increasing the volume of traffic, which in turn made moving drug shipments easier.

Drug trafficking in Central America tends to be a decentralized operation, with drug shipments being passed along a chain of relatively autonomous units, which all take a cut by making money distributing a share of the drugs locally. Cocaine consequently began to be traded in Barrio Luis Fanor Hernández from the mid-1999 onwards, initially on a small scale by just one individual but rapidly expanding into a three-tiered pyramidal drug economy by the first half of 2000. At the top of the pyramid was the '*narco*' – also known as '*el más grande*' ('the biggest') or '*el poderoso*' ('the powerful one') – who brought cocaine into the neighbourhood 'by the kilo', according to several of my informants.[8] The *narco* only wholesaled his goods, among others to the half a dozen '*púsheres*' in the neighbourhood. *Púsheres* resold the cocaine they bought from the *narco* in smaller quantities or else 'cooked' it into crack which they then sold from their houses – '*expendios*' – to a regular clientele that included '*muleros*', the bottom rung of the drug-dealing pyramid. *Muleros* sold crack in small doses to all comers on *barrio* street corners, generally in the form of '*paquetes*' costing 10 córdobas (US$0.70) each and containing two 'fixes', known as '*tuquitos*'.

In total, the Barrio Luis Fanor Hernández drugs pyramid directly involved twenty-nine individuals: one *narco*, nine *púsheres* and nineteen *muleros*. The *narco*, *púsheres* and *muleros* all originated from the *barrio*, and interestingly were all gang members or ex-gang members, or else linked to the latter. Sixteen of the nineteen *muleros* were members of the local youth gang – the '*pandilla*' – and the other three were ex-gang members. The *narco* was an ex-gang member from the early 1990s and all the *púsheres* were either ex-gang members from the mid-1990s or else partners of ex-gang members (all the *muleros* were males, as was the *narco*, but two of the *púsheres* were women). The *narco* and *púsheres* often hired people – generally members of their household – to help them out, but a large number of *barrio* inhabitants were also indirectly involved in the drug economy, acting as '*bodegueros*', stashing drugs in their houses for the *narco* or for *púsheres* in exchange for payment (the *narco* or *púsheres* spread their stocks of drugs in different places in order to keep only easily disposable quantities in their homes in case of a police raid – although this was an extremely rare occurrence, and corrupt policemen would often provide tip-offs – but in this way they also involved other households in the trade and minimized the risk of denunciation).

Bodegueros were generally paid between 200 and 1,000 córdobas (US$15–70) to stash drugs, depending on the quantity and the length of time they had to be stored, which constituted a substantial sum of money in a context where the median wage was about 1,500 *córdobas* (US$105). Those more directly involved in the drugs trade made much more, however. But at the top of the pyramid, although the *narco*'s profits from drug dealing were clearly very substantial, we are not talking about the multi-million sums associated with the drugs trade in the popular imagination. I have little specific information to offer about either the *narco* or the *púsheres*' profits, but it was obvious from their consumption patterns that both made sizeable profits. The former clearly made much more than the latter, however. The *narco* could afford two houses in the neighbourhood – where he maintained a wife and a mistress, as well as half a dozen children, in affluent style – one in a neighbouring *barrio*, another in a richer part of the city, and he had built a new house for his parents, who were living in the neighbourhood. Moreover he owned a fleet of eight taxis, as well as two more cars for his own personal use, and a couple of large motorcycles. Furthermore, the *narco* also regularly bestowed favours on his immediate neighbours by distributing free food and lending them money interest free or at a reduced rate compared to market prices.

The *púsheres* publicly flaunted their wealth by building gaudy, ostentatious houses frequently painted in bright colours – yellow, spearmint green, pink – which more often than not had extravagant fittings – in one case, crystal chandeliers (hanging from a corrugated-iron roof) – and exotic furniture such as rococo full-length mirrors, as well as luxurious home appliances such as wide-screen televisions, mega-wattage sound systems and Nintendo game consoles. Almost all owned at least one car, and some had two homes, one to live in and one to sell their drugs from. *Púsheres* also often wore obviously expensive brand-name clothes – Lacoste, Polo Ralph Lauren, Benetton – gold jewellery and luxury watches, and made a point of drinking costly drinks such as whisky instead of rum, smoked foreign-brand cigarettes, and shopped in Managua's two supermarkets rather than in the markets, thereby differentiating themselves from the rest of the *barrio* population. Interestingly, the *narco* somewhat paradoxically cut a rather shabby figure in comparison to the *púsheres*. He generally dressed down, and rarely wore gold jewellery or other items of obvious luxury. He frequently flaunted his wealth in other ways, however. While neither of his houses in the neighbourhood was as ostentatious as those of *púsheres*, both the one he built for his parents and the one he had in the neighbouring *barrio* were two-storey buildings – a rarity in Barrio Luis Fanor Hernández and indeed in Managua more generally. Furthermore, the *narco* would also regularly drive through the neighbourhood on one of his motorcycles, notoriously accosting passing women – whether single or not – and offering them substantial sums of money to sleep with him, thereby signalling his power and impunity within the strictures of machismo that frame so much of social life in contemporary Nicaragua (see Montoya 2003).

Although the *narco* and the *púsheres* obviously moved greater quantities of drugs, even at the lowest level of the drug dealing pyramid, that of the *muleros*, the rewards were potentially substantial. *Muleros* bought crack from *púsheres* in the form of *tucos*, nuggets about the size of the first phalange of the thumb, for 500 córdobas (US$36) each. They would then cut (*'picar'*) the *tucos* into *tuquitos* – each *tuquito* was about 2 square millimetres in size, with a variable weight of 0.10–0.50 grams – which they would then wrap in aluminium foil, and put into *paquetes* of two. Each *paquete* was sold for a standard price of 10 córdobas (US$0.70). On average, a *mulero* would sell forty to fifty *paquetes* a day, with peaks of eighty to one hundred *paquetes* on Fridays and Saturdays, and lows of ten to twenty on Sundays.[9] Each *tuco* bought for 500 córdobas would yield between 160 and 190 *tuquitos*, depending on the *mulero*'s cutting skills and also how much he kept for his own consumption. This in turn corresponded to eighty to ninety-five *paquetes*, which given that these sold at 10 córdobas each meant that the profit on each 500-córdoba outlay was between 300 and 450 córdobas (US$22–32), although 12 córdobas have to be discounted for a roll of aluminium foil, and a further 5 córdobas for the small plastic bags in which *muleros* put the *tuquitos*.

In other words, at the bottom of the drug-dealing pyramid, a *mulero* could make between 5,000 and 8,500 córdobas (US$350–600) profit per month, equivalent to between three and five times the average Nicaraguan wage; as such, it can be contended that low-level drug dealing constituted one of the most profitable economic opportunities available to youth at the local level. Like the *púsheres*, albeit more modestly, the *muleros* generally sported good-quality clothes – often global brand names such as Nike, for example – as well as gold chains, rings and also Walkmans and portable CD players. They would in addition spend considerable amounts of money on cigarettes and alcohol, although generally local brands only rather than foreign goods, in contrast to the *púsheres*. At the same time, however, similarly to the *púsheres*, the *muleros* devoted substantial proportions of their wealth to improving the material conditions of their households, and also those of their extended families in the *barrio*. In a neighbourhood that was over forty years old, this meant that the trappings of drug-fuelled economic development extended far beyond just those directly involved in the trafficking, to the extent that from a nucleus of about thirty individuals up to 40 per cent more households in Barrio Luis Fanor Hernández were visibly better off than in non-drug-dealing neighbourhoods. For those who did not fall in the 40 per cent of neighbour-hood households that were better off, however, life seemed to continue much as it had in the mid-1990s.

Consumption, cultural exclusion and predation

In a recent article describing how the illegal drugs trade affected and transformed the rural small-town community of Buenavista in the central highlands of Mexico, McDonald (2005: 120) argues that a drug economy can be 'a powerful source of cultural as well as economic change through the routinized forms of everyday cultural practice that lead to transformations of existing activity, organization, and identity'. In particular, McDonald contends that the cultural routinization of the drugs trade in Buenavista – as reflected in the proliferation of particular architectural forms (opulent housing), the presence of luxury commodities (expensive cars and designer clothes) and the adoption of non-traditional patterns of consumption (high-stake betting at cockfights) – has generated inequalities that go beyond simple quantitative differences in material wealth. Drawing on Appadurai (1996), he maintains that although consumption is obviously an important economic process, it is even more critical as a cultural practice through which people constitute and define themselves as social beings, and that – implicitly arguing that they constitute a class of 'cultural entrepreneurs' – the emergent drug-dealing elite in Buenavista and their new patterns of consumption have become the primary source of symbolic inspiration for the construction of local identities in the community, thereby reshaping it 'in subtle and not so subtle ways' (McDonald 2005: 117).

Obvious among these changes are the adoption of new consumer practices by local community members not involved in the drugs trade, more and more of whom seek to adopt the trappings of a drug-trafficking lifestyle that is seen to epitomize the apex of social accomplishment, for example buying what they can in the way of designer clothes and sartorially imitating drug dealers. But what these signal at a less apparent underlying level are fundamental

79

transformations of what can be termed – after Taylor (2002) – the 'local social imaginary'. The new consumption patterns of the drug-dealing elite alter notions of what it is to imagine and to be a member of the community, and this leads to what McDonald (2005: 118) refers to as 'slippage'. The drug-dealing elite and non-drug-dealing members of the local community enter into acts and rituals of consumption differently, and find themselves as a result starkly distinguished from one another. Although both groups imagine their identities through the same forms of consumption, only the former can actually afford them, meaning that the latter are constantly reminded of what they lack, and end up feeling an acute sense of relative deprivation, or, to put it another way, find themselves culturally excluded. From this perspective, the rise of the drugs trade and the associated conspicuous consumption patterns of drug dealers can be said to generate powerful forms of social disjuncture within the local community that go far beyond the solely material.

Such an analysis is very attractive when one considers Veblen's (1902) original characterization of the notion of 'conspicuous consumption', whereby he maintains that it is a process that revolves primarily around socio-cultural differentiation rather than material wealth. Indeed, Veblen (ibid.: 68) actually argues that 'the beginning of a differentiation in consumption even antedates the appearance of anything that can fairly be called pecuniary strength'. There is evidence to suggest that this is perhaps true in the case of Barrio Luis Fanor Hernández, where the drugs trade was intimately associated with the local gang. Certainly, the gang in the 1990s had constituted a locus of particular social practices such as binge drinking, smoking marijuana and wearing Nike shoes that could arguably be seen as progenitorial to contemporary forms of conspicuous consumption, although it should be noted that gang members were far from being in any way wealthy (see Rodgers 2006). Moreover, the better-off part of Barrio Luis Fanor Hernández – the *'arriba'* side – corresponded spatially more or less exactly to what had been in the mid-1990s the territory of the age cohort of the gang that became the nucleus of the gang in 2002. At the same time, this association is perhaps most interesting when considered in the light of Veblen's claim that differentiation is ultimately traceable back to what he calls 'predatory culture'. From this perspective, the political economy of the violence that surrounds the drugs trade in Barrio Luis Fanor Hernández becomes particularly significant.

Violence and primitive accumulation

By all accounts the neighbourhood had become a much more violent place since the development of a drugs economy. To a certain extent, this was due to the neurological effects of crack consumption. Crack enhances aggressiveness, and makes individuals less predictable. As a *barrio* inhabitant called Adilia explained to me: 'The problem is that now, anybody could be a potential danger, if they've smoked some crack, any time … you can't know what they're going to do, with this drug people become more violent, more aggressive, they don't care about anything, they don't recognize you … you don't know what they're thinking or even if they're thinking at all, they could just kill you like that, without a thought … '

Everybody I talked to in Barrio Luis Fanor Hernández told me without exception that insecurity had worsened since the emergence of crack, and in particular that there had been an increase in brutal robberies, assaults and common delinquency. This was certainly supported by my observations of everyday *barrio* life during my return visit in 2002, when it was apparent that there were more acts of spontaneous, unpredictable violence occurring on a daily basis than in the mid-1990s. These were indeed more often than not linked to crack consumption. It was extremely frequent to see drugged-up individuals stopping neighbourhood inhabitants in the streets of the *barrio* and asking for a few córdobas to buy another fix. If their request was refused or ignored, they would frequently become violent, lashing out with a fist, pulling out a knife or wildly swinging a machete. Indeed, weapons such as knives and machetes, but also guns – I witnessed four shoot-outs during the course of two months in the *barrio* in 2002 – were used much more frequently than in the past, and often openly carried about, which had not been the case previously.

At the same time, although crack consumption was clearly important in explaining these increased levels of violence and insecurity, it can also be argued that these were to a larger extent a consequence of the nature of the drugs trade itself. A drug economy cannot rely on formal mechanisms of regulation and contract enforcement such as the law owing to the fact that drugs are illicit goods. Alternative informal mechanisms are necessary in order to impose regularity on drug transactions, and as has widely been pointed out within the social sciences, perhaps the most basic form of social regulation is achieved through the use and threat of violence. Seen in this way, it was no accident that the drugs trade became dominated by members or ex-members of the local gang. Indeed, in many ways it can in fact be argued that there existed something of a 'contingent compatibility' between the gang and the drugs trade (see Rodgers forthcoming). As a small, tightly-knit group that was the dominant source of violence in the neighbourhood – to the extent that it held a quasi-monopoly over public forms of brutality and fundamentally organized local-level social life in the *barrio* as a result – the gang was well placed to provide the brutal forms of informal regulation required for sustainable drug trafficking when drugs first arrived in the neighbourhood.

Although *mulero* gang members conducted their drug dealing on an individual basis, the gang as a group acted in a coordinated manner to ensure the proper functioning and protection of the *barrio* drug economy, providing security services to the *narco* and to the *púsheres*, and making certain that transactions proceeded smoothly. Gang members would enforce contracts, roughing up recalcitrant clients, as well as guarding drug shipments as they were moved in and out of the *barrio*. They would also make sure that clients could enter the neighbourhood unmolested by either the local population or outsiders. Neighbourhood inhabitants, however, lived under a veritable regime of terror. Gang members would strut about the streets, menacingly displaying their guns and machetes, repeatedly warning *barrio* inhabitants of the potential retribution that would befall them if they denounced them or others involved in the drugs trade, and backing these threats with violence. On one occasion in March 2002, the gang beat up the son of an elderly neighbourhood inhabitant who lived next to a *púsher*, as a warning after she had harangued and thrown a bucket of water on crack buyers who had knocked on her door by mistake late one night.

Seen in this light, the intimate relationship between violence and drug trafficking in Barrio Luis Fanor Hernández potentially points to the latter being a process that bears comparison with Marx's (1976) famous notion of 'primitive accumulation'.[10] According to Marx, capitalism was at its most basic founded upon a unique social relationship between two opposing but inescapably linked social groups: on the one hand a class of capitalists with a virtual monopoly over the means of production, and on the other hand a property-less proletariat that had been dispossessed of their means of production and subsistence, and consequently had only their labour as a resource. The necessary pre-condition for capitalist development was therefore the differentiation of society into these two social classes, and 'primitive accumulation' was the expression Marx used to designate the means through which this differentiation occurred. This generally involved the burgeoning capitalist class violently dispossessing embryonic proletarians of their means of production in order to be able to exploit the labour that they are then subsequently forced to sell in order to survive. The analogy with the Barrio Luis Fanor Hernández drugs economy is not perfect because the drug-dealing elite was not exploiting the local population in the way Marx envisioned capitalists exploiting the proletariat. It is nevertheless worth thinking about in view of the extensive process of socio-economic differentiation that occurred in the *barrio* owing to the drugs trade, and the fact that – following McDonald (2005) – drug trafficking can be seen as transforming the basis of consumption-based local social imaginaries in a way that amounts to a form of symbolic dispossession. The larger question such an analysis raises, however, is why such a process of 'primitive accumulation' should occur in a neighbourhood like Barrio Luis Fanor Hernández, which is theoretically already integrated within the wider Nicaraguan economy.

In this respect, it is illuminating to turn to Davis's (2004; see also 2006) recent work on 'urban involution' and the rise of an informal global proletariat, where he describes the way in which most cities are now principally made up of slums populated by a vast underclass that is increasingly excluded from contemporary production processes and left to survive by its own devices. These are the inevitable flipside of the existence of 'fortified enclaves', where the affluent have decided to live in 'splendid isolation', and constitute 'a fully franchised solution to the problem of warehousing the twenty-first century's surplus humanity' (Davis 2004: 28) in an age of technology and information-based economies. Davis goes on to ask the obvious question as to whether these 'slums of exclusion' are not 'volcanoes waiting to erupt', and suggests that a range of responses are potentially possible, from the emergence of 'some new, unexpected historical subject' that will challenge the process of urban segregation that has been imposed from above to 'ruthless Darwinian competition' within the slums, 'as increasing numbers of poor people compete for the same informal scraps, ensur[ing] self-consuming communal violence as yet the highest form of urban involution'.

What the case study presented in this chapter suggests is that it is the latter option which seems to emerge. The processes in Barrio Luis Fanor Hernández described above have to be situated within the larger context of the top-down process of urban segregation that has occurred in Managua (see Rodgers 2004a). The process of 'disembedding' of the city has not only separated an autonomous 'layer' of the metropolis for the rich, but has also created large 'zones of exclusion' where the impoverished city masses attempt to survive as best they can. A Hobbesian social order has arguably emerged within these zones, where the principal concern of those inhabiting them is material survival, and only the strongest and fittest can attempt to establish means of enrichment that go beyond mere subsistence, for example through violent economic practices such as drug trafficking (indeed, this is perhaps a particularly appropriate way of conceptualizing drug trafficking considering that it is a paradigmatic form of 'savage' capitalism – something that also makes the link to a putative process of 'primitive accumulation' all the more attractive). From this perspective, the drugs trade in Barrio Luis Fanor Hernández constitutes an attempt to create a form of economic organization that goes beyond mere survival in a context of rampant poverty and enforced isolation from the wider social unit of the city.

Conclusion

This chapter has explored what might be termed forms of 'urban segregation from below'. Drawing on a case study of a poor Managua neighbourhood called Barrio Luis Fanor Hernández, I focused on the way in which the emergence of a local drug economy led to significant forms of socio-economic differentiation, which were particularly well reflected in the new conspicuous consumption of drug dealers that have changed local cosmologies and symbolic frameworks. As important as consumption behaviour may be, however, as Rothstein (2005: 298) points out – citing Douglas and Isherwood (1979: 4) – 'consumption has to be set back into the social process'. Although differentiation can be elaborated through consumption, it is ultimately created outside consumption, and therefore 'consumption practices must be viewed in terms of class, political economy and material reality' (Rothstein 2005: 283). In this regard, it is illuminating to consider the process of micro-level social differentiation and economic development that I observed in Barrio Luis Fanor Hernández through the lens of Marx's notion of 'primitive accumulation', the primary characteristic of which is the violent separation of society into capitalists and proletariat, through the former dispossessing the latter of their means of production. Although the analogy is not perfect, it allows us to think more broadly about why the drugs trade has emerged at the micro-level in urban Nicaragua, in essence as an attempt to establish a viable form of economic livelihood that goes beyond mere subsistence.

In many ways, the emergence of such desperate forms of micro-level economic organization is not surprising considering Nicaragua's macroeconomic predicament, which according to Robinson (1998) can be labelled a state of 'mal-development'. Certainly, the country has been caught in a vicious cycle of economic stagnation, suffering severe and increasing disequilibria relative to the global economy. The economy is structurally constrained given its import and export structure, imports having a high inelasticity of demand, while exports have a high elasticity of demand. Traditional export sectors are moreover increasingly uncompetitive in a hemispheric context where there are few possibilities for the development of new export sectors (all the more so following the Central American Free Trade Agreement). To this extent, it can be contended that poor Nicaraguans – because the country's elite is to a large extent transnational in its economic foundations, and controls the few national resources there are – have few options other than to develop non-traditional forms of capital accumulation such as drug trafficking if they are to achieve any form of 'development' that goes beyond simple survival. Whether such strategies will lead to more extensive forms of economic development, however, in the way Marx envisaged 'primitive accumulation' giving rise to capitalism, remains to be seen.

Notes

1 Similar processes have been observed in Buenos Aires (Svampa 2001), Mexico City (Fischer et al. 2003), Lima and Quito (Borsdorf 2002), and Santiago de Chile (Sabatini and Arenas 2000; Salcedo and Torres 2004), among others.

2 A pseudonym, as are all the names of people mentioned in this chapter. Certain factual details have also been changed in order to protect the anonymity of the neighbourhood.

3 The first period of fieldwork was carried out between July 1996 and July 1997 within the context of a social anthropology PhD programme at the University of Cambridge (see Rodgers 2000). The second period was conducted in February/March 2002 as part of the London School of Economics Crisis States Programme, which also sponsored a further visit in December 2002–January 2003.

4 On the Sandinista government's urban reconstruction programme, see Drewe (1986) and Vance (1985).

5 In many ways, this situation was arguably worse than it would have been had the neighbourhood not been rebuilt, as cracked paths and drains made of concrete are more difficult to repair than dirt roads and hand-dug drainage ditches.

6 The *barrio* had a population of approximately 3,000 inhabitants and was made up of 369 households. My survey sample was made up of 403 individuals in fifty households.

7 Cocaine is usually distributed either as cocaine hydrochloride powder or as chunky nuggets – known as 'crack' – that are a mix of cocaine and sodium bicarbonate boiled in water. Crack is much less expensive than cocaine powder, and is known as 'the poor man's cocaine'.

8 The *narco* originally came from Bluefields, which is the principal first trans-shipment point on mainland Nicaragua for drugs coming from Colombia via the island of San Andrés. He still had family there, and his supply networks were based on these.

9 A significant proportion of clients were local *barrio* inhabitants, but the vast majority came from outside the neighbourhood, and included both rich and poor Nicaraguans, as well as a trickle of foreigners. Most clients came after nightfall, although a substantial number came during the day, and there was a definite predominance of men over women.

10 I am grateful to Jo Beall for pointing out this analogy.

6 | Caracas

ROBERTO BRICEÑO-LEÓN

For decades, Caracas was considered to be a tranquil and safe city in a country where violence was not a major problem. During the 1980s and early 1990s, Caracas recorded an average of less than one homicide a day. Ten years later, this figure has risen to more than six. In 1990, a total of 2,474 murders were committed in the whole of Venezuela. Twelve years later, in the city of Caracas alone, 2,436 homicides took place. That is to say, in 2002 a similar number of people were murdered in Caracas as were murdered in the entire country a decade earlier. What happened in Caracas and Venezuela that can explain such a drastic change? How has this situation affected life in this erstwhile tranquil city?

Divided Caracas

Caracas is located in a high and cool valley at an altitude of nearly 1,000 metres. It is separated from the sea by a high mountain range that formed a natural protective barrier against the pirates of the Caribbean in the past and against hurricanes up till the present. Until the start of the twentieth century it was a small town, but the arrival of oil wealth set in motion an unexpected process of urban expansion. Like other Latin American cities in the nineteenth century, Caracas used to be the place of residence of large land-owners and export–import merchants. These were few and not very wealthy, however, because Venezuela did not have gold or silver and the exportation of coffee, cocoa and stork plumes – the main sources of foreign income for centuries – was handled through other port cities such as Maracaibo and Ciudad Bolivar. Hence Caracas did not expand; the city lacked large churches and monumental buildings.

Constructed according to the chequer-board grid pattern, Caracas followed faithfully the urbanization instructions of Philip II. The city's growth took place on the river banks, that is to say newcomers built their houses expanding the grid outwards, slowly adding one block after another, preserving the grid pattern. This pattern of urban growth continued until a physical obstacle, such as a mountain or a river, halted further extension. At the city's edges, on the river banks or in the areas beyond rivers or bordering bridges, the danger-ous parts of the city could be found. Here lived the newly arrived migrants, the poor; here the ill-reputed bars and brothels were located. The excluded zones of the city were situated on the river banks (*orillas*), hence the term *orillero*, meaning a poor, uneducated and possibly dangerous individual.

This pattern of growth persisted until the 1930s when rural–urban migration started to accelerate as a result of the mechanisms of distribution of oil revenues (Chen et al. 1986). The worldwide capitalist crisis had a profound effect on Venezuela because, whereas other countries devalued their currencies in order to support continued exports, Venezuela revalued its currency and put an end to the export of agricultural products that traditionally sustained the economy. This was possible owing to the fact that oil revenues had become the principal source of state income. From that point onward oil and the central state came to dominate the economy and the process of urban expansion (Baptista 1997, 2004). The basis of Caracas's urban economy changed from the rents obtained by the landowners to the resources received and distributed by the national government.

In 1941 Caracas had 358,000 inhabitants. Forty years later, its population had increased tenfold, and in 2000 the city housed 3,353,000 inhabitants, not counting the more than 1 million suburban residents who worked in the city (Negrón 2001). This increased population found space in different parts of the valley as a result of distinctive patterns of settlement that involved three types of actors: central and local government, private sector urban project developers, and informal occupants. These three actors have been constructing present-day Caracas either separately or in combination, leading to various patterns of territorial inclusion and exclusion (Briceño-León 1986).

Private sector urban developers have progressively transformed the sugar cane and cocoa estates that occupied the eastern part of the Caracas valley into urbanized lots for the construction of individual dwellings for the rich and the new middle class created by employment in the public sector and urban services. The state also built, put water and sewerage systems in place, laid out streets and the highway system of the city. But the state also provided housing areas for low-income sectors in the form of small lots and houses (San Augustín) or high-rise apartment buildings (Lídice, 23 de Enero), or even in the form of complete urban development areas such as in the central zone, where various hectares of run-down houses and bordello zones were replaced by fancy residences, shops and offices. Territorial occupation by the formal actors of the state or the private developers was followed, however, by the illegal territorial occupation of the 'informal developers', who occupied the spaces close to where the public services could be found. Large-scale immigration into the city brought not only professionals and the middle class

Caracas

87

but also large numbers of construction workers who were building the city but did not have a place to live there. Since the formal housing market did not provide it, they found it themselves, building in the spaces that were left open by the other two actors: the ravines or the distant hill slopes (Acosta and Briceño-León 1987).

The expansion of the city therefore followed a pattern of segmentation: on the one hand in the formal spaces produced by the state and the private sector; on the other hand in the informal spaces built by the squatters (*pobladores*) themselves (Bolívar and Baldó 1995). These urban spaces were united and separated in three different models. The first model is that of 'proximity-distance' where the division between the formal and the informal sector is formed by either a natural barrier (such as the Guaire river that separates formal San Augustín from informal Charneca) or a man-made barrier (such as the motorway that separates the middle-class zone of La Urbina from the informal zone of Petare). The second model is that of the 'enclave', where a poor and informal population takes residence on unused hillsides or river banks within high-income areas. In the third model, the least common, the distinction is not physical or spatial but strictly legal, based exclusively on the prevalent situation of land ownership. Parcels owned by the state or without clearly defined titles were occupied by the informal urbanizers.

The result has been that there are two cities that are coexisting in a way that is at the same time integrated and separated. We cannot say that there is a marginal city that is isolated from the other city. Both coexist and are interdependent, but in a segregated way. In one part of the city, residents do not own the land on which their houses are built, nor have they registered formal ownership of their dwelling, nor do they pay for water, garbage collection or urban taxes. In the other part of the city residents are private owners of terrain and housing and they pay service costs and sometimes taxes. Both faces of the same city exemplify different job markets and different manifestations of state presence and the rule of law. Caracas is a fragmented city that deals with crime and violence in differential modes.

The advent of violence in Caracas

External oil revenues enter Venezuela through the central government, which distributes these resources in unequal form among the various regions of the country. In certain areas, such as Caracas, money has historically been spent in abundance. Other areas, where much less money is spent, constitute the zones of inclusion and exclusion of the distributive circuits of Venezuelan oil income (Briceño-León 1991). As a result of being the seat of the central government and of the country's elite, Caracas experienced a sustained process of urban growth and social improvement until the 1980s. Until that time, the violence in the city was limited. During the 1960s, influenced by the Cuban revolution, a group of political activists started a guerrilla movement with limited urban presence because its actions were concentrated in the rural areas until its demise there thanks to the military and agrarian reform. The urban wing of the guerrilla movement carried out a few terrorist attacks and tried to sabotage the presidential elections in Caracas, but its impact was very small and did not affect city life, which enthusiastically witnessed the pacification of the guerrillas.

A decade later, in the mid-1970s, the Middle East declared an oil embargo, oil prices tripled and Venezuela went through a tremendous economic bonanza and period of euphoria. This was translated into accelerated urban growth, expansion of the construction sector and a new wave of national and foreign immigrants that intensified the patterns of territorial occupation described above. The occupational density of middle-class zones increased and territorial expansion of new neighbourhoods served the poor who came from other parts of Venezuela, but also from Colombia, Ecuador and Peru. These migrants were seeking better job opportunities as, at the end of the 1970s, the wage of a domestic worker in Caracas was comparable to an engineer's salary in Lima. In this context violence was associated with the conflicts related to the social integration of the newcomers, with increased thefts and robbery, but a significant increase in homicides or other crimes against persons did not take place (Ugalde 1990). This situation started to change after 1980 owing to shifts in the dynamics of oil income. The immense oil-derived wealth changed into poverty within a brief period of time, causing the downfall of the elaborated model of revenue distribution and rent-seeking. Having known a money convertibility currency, a fixed exchange rated that endured almost twenty years and an overvalued currency that allowed for the import of almost everything the country consumed, Venezuela was suddenly forced to adopt a policy of currency control and devaluation. These policies were adopted on 'Black Friday' in February 1982, but in effect the slowdown in private investment, the increase of the foreign debt and the deterioration in workers' real incomes went back to 1980 (despite the unprecedented levels of oil income at that time). Economic measures imposed exchange rate and price controls as well as job stability but did not succeed in containing the fall in real wages nor the deterioration in living standards that opened the doors to violence.

Early in 1989 a new government led by Carlos Andres Pérez came into office. During the previous months price controls for basic consumer goods had caused artificial scarcity owing to stockpiling by merchants. Everything from spice oil, sugar and coffee to tissues had to be bought on the black market. The new government rekindled the image of abundance because the president had served a first term during the years of opulence. The population expected an immediate improvement, but one of the first measures of the new government was to increase the gasoline price, leading to a tariff rise in public transportation. On 27 February 1989 passengers coming from a town close to Caracas started to protest against the fare rise. The protest rally erupted into violence but the government, less than a month in office, decided not to take repressive action. In a matter of hours the protest had spread all over Caracas; the dissatisfaction with the rise in transport tariffs unleashed the pent-up anger caused by the scarcity of staple foodstuffs that in turn was created by the combination of price controls and stockpiling. The looting was televised and showed a violence never seen before that was soon repeated in many parts of the city. The police failed to act and shop-owners started to defend their properties, but it proved impossible to halt the avalanche of looters. Two nights of violence and partying in many areas of the city followed, until the military went in to restore order. At that moment, many of the inhabitants of the poor neighbourhoods that were close to the looting feared that the plundering would be extended to their homes, since there was no controlling force; people were terrified by the prospect of anomie and madness. After a week of violence the Caracas morgue contained 534 dead (Briceño-León 1990). The casualties were the result of confrontations with the police, quarrels among looters, the repressive actions of the army, or stray bullets, as in the case of a woman who was killed by a bullet while watching the frenzy from her thirteenth-storey apartment balcony.

Until 1989 the homicide rates in Venezuela and Caracas in particular were stable. Although the Caracas rates were slightly higher, the increase or decrease in both figures followed the same pattern and always maintained the same proportions. But after 1989 this pattern changed as the capital experienced a steep rise in homicide rates not reflected in the rest of the country. Outside Caracas, rates declined, demonstrating the episodic nature of the violence caused by the 1989 violent protests in Caracas known as the *caracazo* (Pérez Perdomo 2002; Sanjuán 1997). Three years later Caracas again became the scene of violent confrontations. This time, however, not poor citizens but the military were involved, taking up arms against the government in two coup attempts. On 4 February 1992, a group of military that had been secretly conspiring for several years took to the street at midnight with the objective of

TABLE 6.1 Homicides in Venezuela, 1990–2003

	Total homicides	Population (millions)	Rate per 100,000 inhabitants
1990	2,474	19.7	12.53
1991	2,502	20.1	12.38
1992	3,366	20.6	16.29
1993	4,292	21.1	20.32
1994	4,733	21.5	21.92
1995	4,481	22.0	20.32
1996	4,961	22.9	22.04
1997	4,225	23.4	18.40
1998	4,550	23.4	19.43
1999	5,974	23.8	25.02
2000	8,021	24.3	32.99
2001	6,432	24.7	25.97
2002	9,244	25.2	36.65
2003	13,288	26.0	50.96
2004	Publication of the data prohibited		

Source: Author's elaboration of data from the Cuerpo de Investigaciones Científicas Penales y Criminalísticas of the Instituto Nacional de Estadísticas.

occupying the government palace and the presidential residence. Confrontations between rebellious and loyal soldiers ensued; the fighting took place in residential areas where fear-stricken families couldn't believe their eyes. The several dozens of victims came from both the contending groups and the citizenry. At daybreak, coup leader Lieutenant Colonel Chávez surrendered in front of the television cameras. The instability did not abate, however, and in November of the same year Caracas suffered the impact of another coup attempt. Troops again fought each other in the streets as they tried to occupy public buildings and television stations. This time the attack was even more impressive because it was accompanied by air raids mounted by the Venezuelan air force, whose war planes launched their ordnance against the seat of the government and the small airport located in the city centre, as if in a tragic and at the same time burlesque war scenario.

The total number of homicides in the country, which had been stable in the years before the military revolts – 2,474 homicides in 1990 and 2,502 in 1991 – rose to 3,366 in 1992. The homicide rate in Venezuela increased from 12.5 per 100,000 inhabitants in 1991 to 16.29 in 1992 (see Table 6.1). But the more sizeable impact of the 1992 events was not registered in that year but

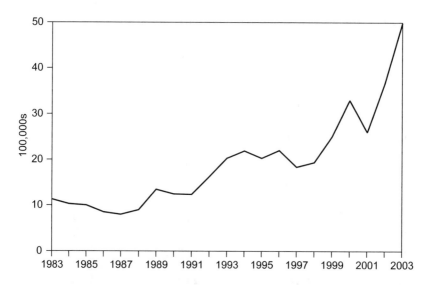

Figure 6.1 Homicide rates in Venezuela, 1983–2003 (per 100,000 inhabitants) (*Source*: Elaborated from Table 6.1)

became manifest during the immense institutional crisis that developed in the country in the years to follow. The increase in homicides in 1992 can be directly attributed to the number of – military and civilian – casualties of the violent confrontations. This explanation does not hold for the following year, however: despite the absence of military skirmishes, homicides continued to go up and, for the first time in the history of the country, exceeded the 4,000 mark in a single year (4,292 in 1993). This increase appears to be the product of the severe institutional crisis that befell the country. The battles among the military, the impeachment of the president of the republic and the ensuing governability crisis immersed Venezuela in a kind of anomie that lasted until an elected president again took office in 1995. From that year onward homicide numbers stabilized at around 4,000 per year without further increase or decrease. This situation continued until 1999, when the country entered a period of political turmoil and the violence situation changed radically (Briceño-León 2005a).

During Lieutenant Colonel Hugo Chávez's 1998 electoral campaign, 4,550 homicides were committed in the country, increasing to 5,974 in the following year; four years later, in 2003, the number of dead victims surpassed 13,000, divided between those described as homicides and those registered as 'resisting the authorities'. As can be seen in Figure 6.1, between 1999 and 2003 a steep and abnormal rise in the homicide rate curve took place. What happened in the country?

From 1999 onward Venezuela entered a complex and confused social and political process characterized by high levels of confrontation between rival groups and by the dual nature of government policy. President Chávez won the elections with a double message for the country. On the one hand, he was a military man representing the notion of 'being tough' on crime and corruption. As a military man he symbolized the classic image of 'law and order' dictatorships. On the other hand he reflected a desire for social change that was supported by a majority of the Venezuelan people. Hence, in his other role Chávez was more of a disorganizer than a stabilizer. This duality was maintained in government action and its responses have been confusing for the population. On the one hand, the president of the republic demonstrated a moderate posture, arguing that it was understandable that people should steal because of hunger. On the other hand, a vice-minister for citizen security declared shamelessly that the police had killed more than two thousand 'pre-delinquents' that year (Briceño-León 2005b). This ambiguity on the part of the state further complicated the difficulties of the rule of law and law enforcement in Venezuela; as such, it forms the foundation of the new violence in Caracas.

Forms of violence

In this context, various types of violence are manifest in Venezuela, particularly in Caracas: criminal violence, youth gang violence, political violence, and violence as a response to violence.

Criminal violence The surprising thing about the new situation in Latin America is not so much the increase in crime but rather the increase in the violent component of crime (Briceño-León 2005c). Crimes against property have always been a problem in the large cities of the region, but these acts used to be committed without violence; the delinquents relied on stealth and skill but hardly ever on the use of force. This situation changed radically when the increase in thefts started to make individuals and businesses protect themselves more forcefully. An outstanding example of this process is provided by car robberies, the second-most important field of action of organized crime after the drugs business. This criminal activity links poor small-time and independent delinquents – who actually steal the vehicles – to a legal, formal, commercial organization that takes care of bringing the stolen cars back on to the market. Stealing cars was basically a non-violent matter until the use of car alarms, mechanical locks and blocking systems became generalized. At that point it proved easier to threaten the driver with

Caracas

a gun to make him or her hand over the vehicle than to try to break into the car. Statistics in Venezuela demonstrate that during the 1990s the number of car thefts (without personal violence) stabilized while the number of car robberies (with personal violence) increased. From 2000 onward, the latter have surpassed the former (Pérez Perdomo 2002).

A second form of urban crime is the so-called 'express kidnappings', a new modality that has developed into an important public security problem in Caracas. Traditional kidnapping has increased as well in Venezuela (more than three hundred victims in 2003) – this is not a problem in Caracas itself but in the border regions with Colombia, where guerrillas and drugs traffickers are active. Express kidnappings are different because victims are held for only a few hours during which they are forced to draw money from their accounts with their bank cards or the family is asked to pay an easily obtainable amount of money. The increase in these types of crimes is related to the use of sophisticated protection systems in private residences and business establishments, but also to the proliferation of automatic money tellers or cashpoints. The advantage of this activity over the traditional stealing of goods is that it immediately yields cash, whereas conventional theft requires intermediaries who buy the goods and sell them for prices below the formal market value. This takes time and effort that can be avoided by the express kidnapping method. Traditional kidnappings, moreover, require complex and costly logistics, which means that they are only feasible with wealthy persons, entailing a limited number of actions that yield high ransoms. Express kidnappings, on the other hand, have very low operational costs, which makes it worthwhile to demand much smaller amounts of money, in turn widening the spectrum of potential victims to include middle-class people; in this case, many actions yield small amounts.

A third very important type of crime in Caracas is the mugging of passengers in public transport. This takes place mostly in the buses that serve the poor districts or use the city's motorways – in other words, places with low vigilance and easy escape routes for the assailants, who normally work in groups of three. Number one threatens the driver at gunpoint and takes his money, number two takes up an armed position at the back of the vehicle, while number three collects money, mobile phones and other valuable objects from the passengers. Such an operation takes a few minutes while the bus is moving. Another, less common method is used during traffic jams on the highways that link Caracas to its suburbs. Cars and buses that are stuck in the congestion fall victim to criminals from adjacent neighbourhoods.

These forms of crime have a large impact on the citizenry, especially on poor people who depend on public transportation. Although the value of the losses is not very high, the events are recurrent and very aggressive; in many cases confrontations between attackers and drivers or passengers result in a considerable number of casualties.

Gang violence The majority of murder victims in Caracas are young poor males (Briceño-León 2003). These youngsters, both victims and victimizers, are members of gangs that are formed in neighbourhoods with a low police presence and absence of the rule of law. The topography of the terrain, with mountain slopes and deep river gullies, accentuates the segregation of these neighbourhoods and facilitates territorial control by the gangs. These operate as defence mechanisms for the juveniles against the potential aggression of other gangs, but also as a resource to exploit the neighbourhood, in particular through storing and retail selling of drugs. The virtual absence of police control, and sometimes police complicity, allows drug consumers or retailers from other parts of town to come in unchallenged. These territories are therefore very valuable and the gangs enter into violent confrontations to control them. This generates among them an endless chain of aggression and vengeance that in Caracas is known as *culebras* (snakes) (Marquez 1999).

Juvenile violence also has a very powerful cultural and symbolic dimension. Economic rationality is not the dominant driving force, at least not for youngsters of twenty for whom violence also means a search for personal identity and a desire to be acknowledged that gives meaning to meaningless lives. In Caracas, 28 per cent of youngsters between the ages of fifteen and eighteen neither work nor attend school (IUCAB 2001). These are juveniles who have dropped out of school but have not yet reached the age that allows them legally to work without parental consent. They strive for consumption patterns that cannot be satisfied with the conventional methods of work and savings. They are the forgotten ones, the redundant ones, and violence converts them into respectable persons (Zubillaga and Briceño-León 2001).

Political violence From the year 2000 onward, a new form of violence emerged in the country: political violence. The internal divisions that were provoked by government plans and actions created a tense climate among the supporters of both the Chávez government and the opposition. Both sectors rallied in two distinct parts of the city: supporters of the government in the historical city centre, and supporters of the opposition in the eastern part. In 2002 and 2003 various demonstrations against the Chávez government were fired on by policemen, sharpshooters or individuals sympathetic to the government. The city of Caracas is divided into five municipalities (*alcaldías*) and a metropolitan administration, each of which has its own police force. Since three municipalities and the metropolitan administration are controlled by the opposition, the central government decided to weaken and disarm these police forces. This political confrontation severely eroded their power and their ability to guarantee citizen security and to fight crime. For the first time in decades, Caracas became the scene of terrorist bomb attacks against several embassies; a controversial civil servant was assassinated in his car. Political violence did not lead to many dead, but its impact in terms of increasing crime and violence is far greater than can be expressed in the number of victims.

Violence in response to violence The response of an important part of the population to this notable increase in violence has been equally violent (Briceño-León et al. 2002). The response is violent in the sense that the possession of firearms or the desire to buy these has increased. In a survey that we conducted in 2004, 47.8 per cent of the respondents said that they would like to own a firearm. It is violent also because of the increase in extra-legal actions by the police and the increase in citizen support for extra-legal action in non-political situations. For instance, in 1996 we asked whether people believed that the police had the right to kill criminals and 32 per cent responded affirmatively (Briceño-León et al. 2003); in 2004 this percentage had risen to 38.

Fear as an urban sentiment

Violence has made fear of being a victim a prevailing sentiment in the city and restraint the common response of the citizens (Ferraro 1995; Soares 1996). In Caracas, fear is more evenly distributed than risk: although major risks exist in the poor parts of town, where the largest number of victims of violence are to be found, fear exists among all social sectors and in every part of the city (Zubillaga and Cisneros 2001).

The results of the surveys that we conducted in 1996 and 2004 show that two-thirds of the population are afraid of being a victim of violence in their own home, half of whom professed to be 'very' afraid (see Table 6.2). In both cases women and married couples demonstrated more fear than men and single persons. The poor (44 per cent) and the lower middle class (46 per cent) demonstrated the most intense fear. Fear in the neighbourhood streets appeared to be at a similar level to fear in the house, but in this case the indices for the lower middle class (49 per cent) and the lower class (42 per cent) were much higher than for the middle class (31 per cent). This seems to be explained by the relative frequency of use made of the street and

TABLE 6.2 Feelings of fear in distinct urban domains, Caracas, 1996 and 2004 (percentage of survey respondents)

Do you feel fear in ...		Caracas 1996 (n: 1,297)	Caracas 2004 (n: 196)	Venezuela 2004 (n: 1,199)
Your house or apartment	Much	36.8	35.6	44.4
	Some	38.6	31.3	29.6
	None	24.6	33.1	25.7
In the streets of your neighbourhood	Much	37.6	45.0	44.0
	Some	35.5	27.5	29.0
	None	25.0	27.5	26.0
Your workplace	Much	26.2	32.0	34.6
	Some	32.9	22.7	29.6
	None	40.9	45.3	35.8
In public transportation	Much	61.0	61.0	56.8
	Some	29.2	27.0	25.6
	None	9.8	12.0	16.2

Source: Author's elaboration of survey data from Laboratorio de Ciencias Sociales, LACSO, 1996, 2004.

public spaces; the poor people travel on foot and use the street frequently as a place for meeting and diversion, while the middle classes go by car and hardly ever use the streets. Fear in public transportation is the highest: in both surveys nine out of ten respondents expressed having experienced fear. Surprisingly, in both surveys 61 per cent said they felt 'much' fear. Again, the poor demonstrate higher indices because it is they who need to use public transport on a daily basis. The workplace appeared to be the place where the largest number of respondents indicated that they felt no fear and where the index of intense fear was lowest. Even here, however, almost half of the respondents nurtured certain apprehensions.

The loss of the city

Fear of violence leads to 'losing the city' because people no longer go to certain areas or leave their homes at certain hours considered dangerous. There are places where you can go and others that are to be avoided. There are hours at which you can leave your house and hours at which you cannot return from a party. And so the city becomes increasingly alien. This process has always occurred in cities, but the magnitude of the inhibition changes from one city to another, from one period to the next.

In Caracas, the violence has had a very strong impact on leisure activities and in shopping areas (see Table 6.3). Leisure has been affected by fear of being assaulted outside at night. Some cinemas have moved performances forward and some cinemas outside shopping malls have cancelled the last performance. In the poor areas of the city, people prefer not to go home after a party, and when they have to do so they prepare an elaborate scheme of family protection, making good use of mobile phones. Historically, the poor zones of Caracas never had fixed telephone services, but the advent of pre-paid mobile phone services caused a spectacular increase in the number of mobile phones. In 1997 there were 1.1 million mobile phones; by 2003 this had risen to 7 million phones among a population of 26 million, that is to say one mobile phone for every 3.7 persons (CONATEL 2004). This increase is due in large degree to the demand of the poor population; one of the principal reasons for buying a mobile phone is personal safety, because it enables one to announce one's imminent arrival in a neighbourhood so that family members or friends can come out in a group to serve as an protective escort.

The restriction of shopping areas has hit certain parts of the city, such as the walkways of Sabana Grande or Catia, and the business of traditional street shops, which have been moving to closed, air-conditioned shopping malls. In the 1970s, when the shopping malls started to proliferate, they were designed for the middle class, but in the new century they have become the preferred shopping areas for everyone, including the poor, who also experience the malls as safe places in which to spend their leisure. This is the reproduction of the street in a private space, protected against the sun and the rain, pleasantly acclimatized but, above all, secure.

People have also restricted their study and work activities, although to a lesser degree (see Table 6.3). This is because, in contrast to leisure or shopping, people have no choice – that is to say, these activities have to be pursued come what may. When people have a certain degree of choice, however, constraints are noted. With respect to education, people limit classroom hours in the evening; the universities, for instance, register a decreasing number of evening students and the classes end earlier because students and professors fear being victimized at the educational facility or when returning home. Something similar happens with respect to work: many employees refuse evening working hours, such as might be entailed by a part-time job, or extra work (although this is more acceptable if it means working all night because this allows one to go home after daybreak).

The principal consequence of fear and inhibition is the loss of the public

TABLE 6.3 Restriction of urban activities due to fear of violence, 1996 and 2004 (percentage of survey respondents)

Restrictions in place or time	Caracas 1996 (n: 1,297)	Caracas 2004 (n: 196)	Venezuela 2004 (n: 1,199)
... when shopping	62.1	63.8	65.8
... when studying	19.0	26.3	32.3
... when working	25.1	30.9	37.1
... in leisure activities	71.8	61.6	58.5

Source: Author's elaboration of survey data from Laboratorio de Ciencias Sociales, LACSO, 1996, 2004.

space. It is lost because people have abandoned it and because it tends to be privatized for security reasons. Very few people in Caracas dare to walk the streets at night, even in the pedestrian areas designed for that very purpose. In this way the cycle is perpetuated because with fewer people these spaces become even more unsafe. But there is also a process of closure of residential streets to limit access to visitors. At first this was undertaken by the middle class, who hired private security, but then the poor neighbourhoods followed suit and closed the walkways with fences and organized in turn their own neighbourhood watch because there was no money to pay others to do the job.

Democracy and violence in the city

Caracas has suffered a process of quite notable deterioration since the 1980s. Until that time the high oil revenues made possible an improvement in the urban quality of life, as well as an increase in real incomes, which had remained constant since the beginning of the 1950s. Towards the areas of informal settlement the state maintained an ambiguous posture of official non-acceptance coupled with a pragmatic acknowledgement of their existence, allowing, supporting or carrying out directly the installation of public services and infrastructure. In a short period of time families were able to improve their dwellings because they had the means to do so; the houses of the poor in Caracas, built with much effort and sacrifice by the *pobladores*, were constantly improved.

This process was halted in the mid-1980s because the statist model that had transformed the government into the entrepreneur behind almost everything slowed private investment and employment. When the oil price fell it

Caracas

proved impossible to finance the oil economy, resulting in a steady decline in real wages to the level they had shown in the 1950s (Briceño-León 2000, 2005b). Subsequently a process of generalized urban deterioration set in, affecting in a particular way the poor areas, however, where a process of urban congestion and decline took shape. Urban congestion was caused by the decreasing availability of urban plots so that growing families resorted to building two, three or even seven storeys on to an already precarious dwelling (Bolívar et al. 1994; Bolívar 1995). Urban deterioration derived from the inability of poor families to maintain their houses, having barely sufficient income for daily sustenance. The state also lacked sufficient resources to maintain the populist policies of distribution. This physical process reversed the sense of urban progress and improvement that prevailed until the 1980s. It put the city in a very difficult predicament of growing unemployment (from 11 per cent in 1998 to 16 per cent in 2004), informality (representing 62 per cent of employment in Caracas) and ungovernability (in various municipalities that are politically challenged).

The failure of the oil economic model brought the country to a political crisis that acquired its own force and dynamics, linking political violence to the complicated situation of personal security. The *caraqueños* (inhabitants of Caracas), like the inhabitants of the other Latin American cities that are beset by violence, are losing their rights to the city. Many people have seen the exercise of full citizenship being limited by poverty and exclusion. Now violence is consolidating new forms of exclusion, constraining even more their access to and use of the city.

For many, natives and immigrants, Caracas was a great dream of social peace and personal advancement. It was a city and a democracy that had been built upon the fragile wealth of oil revenues. It proved to be an illusion that evaporated under the persistence of poverty, inequality and violence.

7 | Lima Metropolitana

DIRK KRUIJT AND CARLOS IVÁN DEGREGORI*

In the late 1980s, the credit card companies informed their clients that they considered three cities, Beirut, San Salvador and Lima, to be the most dangerous urban areas of the world. In those years, Beirut was the theatre of never-ending hostilities between the different guerrilla groups disputing street after street in an enduring civil war. In San Salvador's three international hotels, entire floors were permanently occupied by TV crews reporting day after day the always bloody attacks and counter-attacks between the army and the guerrillas. Lima was a city under siege – at least, that was how the population coped with the car bombs, the intimidation of people's organizations in the working-class neighbourhoods and the executions of local slum leaders and trade union members by Shining Path's assault groups, in a situation where half of the country's territory was declared an 'emergency zone' and the internal war that terrorized the country seemed never ending.[1]

Now, fifteen years later, the internal war over after a decade of rough government under the Fujimori administration, the city is recovering. It still is one of the poorest cities of Latin America: 65 per cent of the economically active population of Lima Metropolitana is employed or self-employed in the informal economy.[2] In terms of security and violence, however, the Peruvian capital appears to be the exception, the deviant case in the roster of Latin American metropolitan cities infested by violence and fear. Although persistent poverty and long-term informality and misery are as manifest as elsewhere in Latin America's capitals, the city is not as overtly contested by armed actors and organized violence as, for instance, Buenos Aires, Caracas, the Central American capitals, Medellín or Rio de Janeiro. In this chapter we aim to clarify this apparent paradox and to explain at least partially the absence of urban governance voids and large-scale violence dominated by state and non-state armed actors. We present our arguments in three sections. In the first we shall follow the economic, spatial and social pattern of the informalization process in Peru, and especially in Lima, with its undermining of the formal entrepreneurial and labour union institutions. This undermining is, however, accompanied by the emergence of a loose network of other popular organizations, less structured, but representing the interests of the 'new inhabitants', the migrants and the informal artisans and self-employed, in the sphere of housing and employment. This is the subject of the second section. In the third part of this chapter we move on to discuss the relative absence of large-scale violence in the four metropolitan cones that together constitute Lima Metropolitana. We also discuss the generalized support of the institutions of law and order in all its urban territory, and the functioning of popular security committees at the *barrio* level. Our principal line of reasoning will be that the overall process of informalization of popular organizations created a tradition of self-help organizations and of alliances with lower-ranking municipal institutions at the *barrio* level. We aim to demonstrate that the format of these popular organizations was transferred from the first generation (habitat organizations) to the second (employment committees) and the third (neighbourhood security institutions).

City of *informales*

Peru's economy, society and political system of the last forty years have been landscaped by consecutive surprise transformations: in the late 1960s and 1970s the 'Revolutionary Government of the Armed Forces', led by the nationalist-leftist military, nationalized significant parts of the economy and organized the urban and rural labour force and small land tenants in cooperatives and unions, federations and confederations. From the early 1980s to the late 1990s a bitter internal war ravaged the indigenous highlands and unsettled the urban slum population. At the end of the 1990s the traditional political parties lost prestige and shrank to near non-existence. In the early 1990s the trade unions, once the bastion of organized labour, virtually disappeared. Fujimori, a kind of 'anti-politician' and keen populist, dominated the political scene during the 1990s as a president with the traits of a civilian and corrupt dictator.[3] Peru's class structure robustly changed, affected by strong demographic, migratory and political transformations. The land reform of the military governments of the 1970s expropriated the rural *latifundista* class. It also initiated, however, a process of mass migration from the rural departments to Lima and other cities. The internal war reinforced this rural exodus and extended it to other urban areas as well, even to secondary cities. The population drain from the highland communities was the principal cause of an explosive expansion of the shanty towns in and around Lima. Between 1960 and 1995 the percentage of indigenous peasants fell from 50 per cent to less than 25 per cent. Parallel with the expansion of the urban population, the informal economy extended into the cities. Until the early 1980s, 65 per cent of the economically active urban

TABLE 7.1 Economically active population (EAP) in Peru (1995)

		Number	%
Receiving wages or salary (29%)	Private sector	1,560,000	18
	Public sector	790,000	9
	Cooperative sector	200,000	2
Not receiving wages (61%)	Urban independents	2,516,000	30
	Peasants	1,200,000	14
	Family workers	700,000	8
	Informal workers	550,000	6
	Domestic workers	260,000	3
Unemployed (10%)		864,000	10
Total EAP		8,640,000	100

Source: Authors' elaboration of data from *Encuesta de niveles de vida en Lima Metropolitana 1970–1993* (ICEI, 1994).

population received a formal wage or salary. In 1995 this percentage was dramatically reduced, which explains the rapid increase in the informal urban economy. Thus, by the mid-1990s the economically active population was largely informalized (Table 7.1).

The volume of the so-called 'urban independents' and of the informal, family and domestic workers is an overall indicator of the growth of the Peruvian informal economy.[4] Over the last fifteen years, four out of every five new jobs have been created in the informal sector. Comparing national census figures for 1971, 1981 and 1993, one can observe a marked increase in female employment: from 34 per cent in 1971 to 50 per cent in 1993. Given the explosion of the informal job market, this phenomenon is to be interpreted as an indicator of the feminization of poverty. Perhaps the most dramatic tendency in the Peruvian economy has been the fall in real income. The average income for the male population in 1993 (in soles constant for 1994 values) was equivalent to 33 per cent of the average income for 1980. In the case of the female population it was 30 per cent. The minimum wage paid in the private sector in 1990 was 41 per cent of its real value in 1980. One can argue, comparing the data from 1990 and 2000, that the configuration of a permanent formal/informal labour market and a related employment structure was consolidated during the 1990s.

These conclusions are corroborated by the data in Table 7.2, showing the evolution and stabilization of Peru's poverty. During the 1990s, the decade of the Fujimori regime with its strict neo-liberal policy, even anchored in

TABLE 7.2 Peru's poverty estimates

Year	Total population (1,000s)	Total poor (1,000s)	Percentages of poor
1985–86	19,490	8,400	43
1991	22,000	12,145	55
1994	23,130	12,350	53
1997	24,370	12,355	51
2000	25,660	13,890	54

Source: Authors' elaboration of survey data reported in Mauro Machuca (2002: 23).

TABLE 7.3 Evolution of minimum urban wages in Peru (1980 = 100)

Year	1992	1993	1994	1995	1996	1997	1998	1999
Lat. Am.	68	68	68	71	70	70	72	73
Peru	16	12	14	15	15	27	30	29

Source: Authors' elaboration of ILO data reported in Webb and Fernández Baca (2001: 105–6).

the constitution of 1993, Peru's poverty figures jumped from around 45 per cent to 55 per cent to remain relatively stable from 1991 to 2000. As shown in Table 7.3, the country's poverty percentages are below those for Latin America as a whole. In 2005, Peruvian cabinet members asserted that this process was 'unstoppable'.[5]

Lima, an elegant city of 500,000 inhabitants until the end of the 1940s, is now, in 2005, a miserable metropolis of more than 8.5 million. The spectacular growth of slums (*barriadas*) and not the steady expansion of the old colonial city centre and the new middle-class neighbourhoods shaped the current four-cone metropolis. Shanty towns, not middle-class resorts, characterize the appearance of the Peruvian capital. In 1957 the inhabitants of the city's 56 *barriadas* accounted for less than 10 per cent of the metropolitan population of around 1,375,000. In 1981 Lima had a total population of around 6 million; 32 per cent of its population lived in the 408 *barriadas*. The estimated population of Lima in 2004 was 8,500,000, of which 5 million, 62 per cent, lived in the *cono norte* (around the northern part of the Pan-American Highway), *cono este* (around the Central Andes Highway) and the *cono sur* (around the southern part of the Pan-American Highway), surrounding the 'old Lima', with its residential middle-class neighbourhoods and its depressing working-class districts.[6]

New social actors and new forms of popular organization

The four *conos* are at least partially integrated. The military governments of the 1970s and the progressive municipal authorities of the 1980s arranged for the construction of internal highways and an intensive transport system of 50,000 buses and 100,000 taxis which, although chaotic and nearly completely informalized under the Fujimori administration in the 1990s, covers the complete territory of Lima. The population of the three new cones is, of course, relatively heterogeneous, being mainly formed by the first and the second generation of provincial migrants. Scraping a living is the lifestyle of most of its inhabitants. Many of the newcomers are self-employed or started with informal enterprises and artisan production in home *talleres*, in-house industrial and commercial activities. Amid the precariousness and the poverty, however, a local 'popular' middle class is arising, an estimated 10 per cent of the population of the northern, central and southern cones (Matos Mar 2004: 134ff.). New commercial establishments and industrial parks emerged in the cones, financed by local investors. In Villa El Salvador, the core of the southern cone and originally a self-management city, the military governments designed an experimental *parque industrial*. Now this industrial zone is consolidated and a complementary commercial plaza with cinemas, restaurants and fifteen bank offices is being constructed. The most spectacular push forward is noticeable in the northern cone, with its Megaplaza, an imposing shopping mall of 125 commercial establishments, attracting more than 1.5 million visitors per month. At night one can dance at one of the fifteen discothèques in another centre of the northern cone, where the sons and grandsons, daughters and granddaughters of the immigrants of the 1960s spend their money. Yet it attracts the public of old Lima, as do the discothèques in the other two cones. The music is outstanding and security problems are absent. We should also mention the existence of Gamarra, an entire industrial district of self-managed and interlinked plants and *talleres* beside La Victoria, one of the oldest and most popular districts of the old Lima. The Gamarra complex encompasses 250–300 street blocks; the buildings are five to eight floors high. Previously its centre, a shopping mall of several blocks, was one of Lima's famous locations for vice, drugs and prostitution. By the end of 1999 this industrial and commercial conglomerate housed around 13,700 small and micro-entrepreneurs, had generated around 60,000 jobs and had a yearly gross sales output of US$800 million. Taxes paid amounted to $140 million that year (Gonzales 2001: 92). The heyday of the Gamarra entrepreneurs was the mid-1990s. At the turn of the century, the Megaplaza and other commercial projects in the northern cone were financed from the revenues of the Gamarra entrepreneurs.

The phenomenon of the *desborde popular* of the *informales*, vividly described by Matos Mar (1984), De Soto et al. (1986) and Carbonetto et al. (1988) in the 1980s, had has long-term consequences for the emergence of a new civil society. The informalization process contributed largely to the decline of the institutional pillars of traditional Peruvian society: the chambers of commerce and industry, the industrial associations, the exporters' associations, the professional colleges of the middle class and the urban trade union movement. The formal organizations of the industrial and commercial entrepreneurs, the lawyers', doctors' and engineers' professional associations and the once all-powerful trade-union confederations dramatically lost membership in the 1980s and stagnated during the 1990s. On the other hand, the informalization process instigated at least three consecutive waves of new popular organizations, representing the interests of the *informales*: the associations of the *pobladores* (slum dwellers) in the 1970s, the association of micro-entrepreneurs and the self-employed in the 1980s and 1990s, and the rural and urban security committees of the 1990s and 2000s. As Degregori et al. (1986) and Golte and Adams (1987) commented with much reason, the new migrants in the slums and the micro-entrepreneurs were poor, unskilled and maybe timid, but they set up their shacks and houses, their commercial outfits and business and their micro-industries with enormous perseverance and assertiveness, using their former Andean family networks and ethos of communal engagement.[7]

The first wave of popular organizations, the associations of slum dwellers, was strongly supported by the military governments (Kruijt 1994: 114ff.). The military even created a ministry (SINAMOS), staffed by the civilian left but also by police detectives and army intelligence, 'to organise the unorganised and to restructure the existing organizations' (Stepan 1978: 158). The government facilitated an elementary service once the land invasion efforts had been successful. SINAMOS staffers and religious leaders advised on the self-management structure of the *pobladores'* associations and federations. The first NGO to emerge in the 1970s assisted as well. The progressive municipal authorities of the 1980s, especially during the municipal government of Barrantes and Peace, created and supported related popular institutions, such as mothers' committees and *comedores populares* (the community-run canteens that provide low-cost food in the *barriadas* of Lima Metropolitana). Women's participation in leadership began to be a regular experience.[8] Around the associations of *pobladores*, the mothers' committees and the self-managed canteens, other institutional networks evolved, forming an overlapping network of popular support organizations in the *barriadas* and working-class neighbourhoods (Riofrío 1990; Driant 1991; Hordijk 2000). The wide expansion of this kind of self-help organizations becomes clear when analysing the phenomenon of the *comedores populares* and the mothers' committees. The authors of a recent study estimate a national total of 16,000 canteens in 2003, of which 10,500 were urban. In Lima Metropolitana there are 6,300 canteens, 40 per cent of the national total. Of the *comedores* in Lima, 60 per cent are self-managed. The female membership surpasses 100,000 and 25 per cent of the women occupy a leadership position at some time. The local significance is very clear: 90 per cent of the female members live in the same neighbourhood (Blondet and Trivelli 2004: 14, 56). At street, block and sector level[9] this kind of association performed and still performs the function of a merger between trade unions and district government. Even the ferocious attacks against the leaders of these neighbourhood organizations by Shining Path during the late 1980s and the early 1990s – around two hundred leaders were executed in Lima Metropolitana – could not break the back of the established working-class networks.

The tentative birth of a diversity of organizations representing micro-entrepreneurs and the informal sector in general – local and regional chambers of craftsmen and semi-institutionalized networks of micro-entrepreneurs and small businessmen – gave way to the second wave of popular organizations. All these organizations for micro-entrepreneurs and the self-employed initially had in common an ambivalent relationship of dependency on professional development organizations: religious or ecclesiastical foundations, NGOs, donor agencies, banks and municipal government institutions assisting civil society organizations (Ypey 2000). Nevertheless, gradually a certain negotiating space in the economic and political domain was established, especially in the industrial *parques* of the 'small and medium businessmen' created in the 1980s for the upper echelon of informal entrepreneurs. Small commercial shops, carpentry and ready-to-wear textile workshops (generally producing imitations of designer garments), inexpensive public transport companies, and restaurants were generally established around these *parques* as a kind of secondary economic activity. The workforce was and is mostly composed of occasional employees, family members, neighbours, acquaintances and migrants from the same place of origin as the entrepreneurs. Real and symbolic kinship relations predominate;

most of the compensation is provided in the form of *comida y casa* (food and accommodation), with no intervention by the authorities, registration of the workers, membership of trade unions or established working hours. The cycle of informal worker becoming micro-entrepreneur is perpetuated: new migrants constitute the new working force under the same conditions. In the case of Gamarra, for instance, 47 per cent of the textile entrepreneurs in 1998 were previously engaged as textile workers and 64 per cent acquired work experience as self-employed informal employees. Of all entrepreneurs, only 20 per cent had received any form of professional training. Of their workers, family ties bound more than 60 per cent. Their average working week is fifty-six hours (Gonzales 2001: 99, 101, 105, 119, 122). A good example of the growing significance of the informal economy is Gamarra, the industrial-commercial complex we mentioned previously. This unregistered micro-enterprise started in the early 1970s in the combined residential/working *talleres* of the new provincial migrants around La Parada, Lima's working-class food and groceries market in the La Victoria district. Street blocks were transformed into *talleres*, thirty or forty per block, constituting generally 50 per cent of the existing space. Industrial self-management inspectors and government labour protection officers were refused entry. Specialized financial institutes (such as the Banco CCC) discovered a potential clientele, however. *Confianza* (personal trust) forms the basis of the relationship between the entrepreneur and the workforce and between members of the entrepreneurial circuit.[10] In fact, 'industrial clusters' of interdependent *talleres* and small service enterprises specializing in a certain sector (textiles, shoes, metallurgy, plastics) with obligatory training and cooperatively administered technology are the typical start-up industries in all three cones. Again, *confianza* relations predominate in the mutual assistance activities. In the northern cone, 99 per cent of the enterprises are the family property of micro-entrepreneurs. The number of micro-enterprises increased during the mid-1990s: from around 13,000 in 1993 to around 33,000 in 1997 (Willer 2005). With the growing importance of the informal economy and society, the political preferences of the *informales* came to be acknowledged. During his presidential campaigns of 1990 and 1995 Fujimori, whose father had a tyre repair shop in La Victoria, presented himself as the champion and spokesman of the *informales* and the poor migrants. His first vice-president in the 1990 campaign, San Román, was a micro-entrepreneur and president of the association of small businessmen. Marquez, his first vice-president after 1995, was the son of a micro-entrepreneur, the first to export blue jeans to the Andean market.

The third wave of popular organizations started off in the late 1980s and early 1990s, and is related to the internal war. The rural population, mostly spontaneously and later assisted by the armed forces, created resistance groups against the guerrilla columns of Shining Path and self-defence organizations to establish law and order in their own communities.[11] These *rondas campesinas*, or self-defence committees, were dissolved in the late 1990s when the military defeat of Shining Path was clearly imminent. Their urban counterparts were the various *comités de parachoque*, neighbourhood security committees collaborating with the local police. The internal war reinforced another security institution, the *serenazgos*, armed nightwatch committees of concerned citizens, in fact a kind of voluntary neighbourhood police force, under the command of the local police commissariat.[12] After the arrest in 1992 of Guzmán, Shining Path's leader, the Fujimori government set up military cleaning squads, army peletons or larger groups including doctors, dentists and social workers to identify and arrest the local Shining Path sympathizers and to restore the confidence of the population in the working-class neighbourhoods and the *barriadas*. It reinforced the creation or continuation of local urban security committees (*comités distritales de seguridad*), whose members keep a close watch on the irregular activities of petty criminals in close cooperation with the local police. In the more elite and middle-class neighbourhoods, and even in some working-class districts, the phenomenon of the local street *guachimanes*[13] (private guardians paid by homeowners and shopkeepers to ensure security) is generalized.

The police force itself, unified in Peru, is subject to an informalization process. In 1990, at the end of the APRA government of Alan García, who regarded the police force as a check on the traditional animosity between the armed forces and the APRA party, the force was expanded to a total of 129,000 officers.[14] In 1997 the force had 120,000 officers. At the end of 2004 the number of police officers was reduced to 90,000 (Perfíl del policía peruano 2004: 55).[15] The reduction in Lima was even more noteworthy: from 30,000 officers in 1997 to 25,000 in December 2004.[16] Given the increase in the urban population one would have expected a police force of around 150,000. The long-term economic depression in Peru that started in the mid-1980s affected the functioning of the police force as well: there is a noticeable shortage of personnel and vehicles. Fuel is rationed to the maximum.[17] Salaries are low, and declining. The police leadership agreed to a kind of self-employment, permitting private guardianship within the context of formal police tasks.[18] Most police officers work on the basis of a '2 to 1' or even a '1 to 1' system: after one or two working shifts as a police officer, they are subsequently employed as private policemen, sometimes still sporting uniform and service pistol. The chief of the police station (*comisario*) has to authorize the employment. Sometimes they negotiate security or protection contracts with construction firms, restaurant owners or industrial and commercial entrepreneurs. This kind of public–private partnership, whatever other effects it may have, at least reduces the necessity of residents of the elite and middle-class neighbourhoods and the tenants of the working-class districts seeking security and protection by other means: through *sicarios* (subcontracted, mostly underage murderers), gangs or armed criminals. Another peculiarity of the police in Lima Metropolitana is the strong overall presence of police stations and patrols – there are no so-called government voids, urban territorial enclaves where the legitimate authority of law and order is absent. The no-go areas are at best a couple of street blocks – certain zones in Callao, Rimac, Barrios Altos and La Victoria. Police stations are established in every district and every *barriada*. In densely populated commercial areas there are *comisarías móviles*, buses transformed into mobile police stations. Gamarra, for instance, has such a mobile station. It has also organized its internal security: licensed porters, vigilantes and patrolmen, paid by the association of proprietors.

Low-intensity violence

In terms of the homicide rate (homicides per 100,000 inhabitants) Lima has a relatively low score, at 25 per 100,000 in 1995, in comparison with the five most homicide-prone metropolitan cities of Latin America: Medellín (248 per 100,000), Cali (112), Guatemala City (101), San Salvador (95) and Caracas (76).[19] Lima's civilian and police authorities and the public in general are much more worried about other sources of violence (Table 7.4). 'Normal' delinquency (street robbery) was mentioned as the principal type of violence in Lima in opinion polls in November 2003. Another frequently mentioned source of violence was aggression by youth gangs. Organized crime is considered to be a lesser threat. At the end of the Fujimori period, during the transition year 2000 and at the start of the Toledo administration, nationwide campaigns against organized crime and criminal gangs were successfully organized. Most members of the criminal leadership were sentenced to long-term imprisonment and the larger criminal bands ceased to exist. Between 2001 and 2004, successive nationwide political campaigns against organized crime and criminal gangs were successfully instituted. Municipal authorities, former members of human rights and research institutes were appointed as minister of internal affairs, vice-minister in charge of the national police, and intelligence chief (Basombrío Iglesias et al. 2004a; Costa and Basombrío

TABLE 7.4 Most common neighbourhood offences, Lima, 2003 (percentages)

Robbery	55
Youth gangs	27
Drug abuse	16
Drugs traffic	1
Murder	0.4

Source: Authors' elaboration of public opinion poll data (October 2003) presented in Basombrío Iglesias (2004: 40).

2003).[20] A police reform was organized, and one of the first results was rising confidence among the metropolitan public in the new police force. In November 2003 32 per cent of the Lima population declared that the police were less corrupt than previously, although 50 per cent thought that the corruption level had not changed (Basombrío Iglesias 2004: 106). Fraud or large-scale corruption is not commonly associated with the police force. The force is chiefly recruited from the working-class neighbourhoods. Generally, police officers spend their years on the force in their own locality. They are considered and consider themselves as members of the civilian population, interested in problem-solving, not in abusive practices. 'The police is not a part of the problem' is the opinion of the political authorities.[21] In all opinion polls of recent years, employment and security are the top priorities mentioned. As is the case in other countries, such as Argentina, the anti-narcotics and anti-kidnapping divisions are de facto 'subcontracted' to the USA. Not only is the Peruvian anti-drugs force completely dependent on intelligence from the CIA, the DEA and the FBI, but their US counterparts provide the technology, the aeroplanes, the uniforms and much of the money for the salary bill. 'In exchange for their supervision, there are no internal drug wars and drug-related paramilitary forces.'[22]

Most of the violence is poverty-related: street robbery, small burglary, neighbourhood dealing in coca and other drugs.[23] In 2003, the police registered 78,750 offences, nearly 50 per cent of the national total. Theft represented 40 per cent, robbery 30 per cent. There were 208 cases of murder and thirteen of kidnapping (Yépez Dávalos 2004: 48). The number of vehicles in the metropolis increased between 1990 and 2005 at a rate of 300 per cent. Nevertheless, the number of car robberies remained stable[24] – an indicator of the relative absence of organized crime. There is organized crime in Lima, but participation fluctuates. Gangs are formed by an ad hoc membership of specialists in arms or equipment. Family ties play a role.

Equipment and sophisticated armament are for hire 'within the circuit'. Penitentiary authorities estimate that there are 250 'specialists' in ad hoc gangs formed for bank robbery and kidnapping.[25] The fact that large-scale or nationwide organized criminality is largely absent is corroborated by penitentiary statistics (Informe Estadístico Noviembre 2004). Those convicted of drug-related criminality total 7,000, a quarter of the national total. They can be divided into three categories: small traders arrested for dealing, *burros* or intermediaries captured during transport activities, and *jefes de banda* (small-scale gang chiefs, around 10 per cent of the prisoners). Another 25 per cent of the prison population is made up of first offenders. More than 40 per cent of all inmates are imprisoned for small-scale robbery, a poverty-related crime. The number of non-adult delinquents quadrupled between 2000 and 2004. There are no statistics concerning imprisoned members of youth gangs.[26] Most Peruvian security analysts consider the problem of this type of gang (*pandillas, barreras* or *pirañas*) as minor in comparison with the Central American countries and Andean countries such as Colombia. Reported youth gang violence is mostly related to territorial disputes between competing *pandilleros* and inter-gang clashes (Mejía 1999: 115–18).[27] Police estimates for 2000 note 390 *pandillas* with eight to fifty members, with a total of 13,000 members in Lima Metropolitana (Yépez Dávalos 2004: 68). Public executions of offenders do occur with some frequency in the working-class districts and slum areas.[28] Generally, however, bystanders call in the police or request the assistance of the local *serenazgo* rather than initiate lynching or corporal punishment.[29]

In terms of overt hostility and brutal behaviour, Lima is a city of relative non-violence. Lima Metropolitana, however, is security conscious. Whereas in the residential areas the phenomenon of gated communities is expanding, in the working-class districts spontaneous security associations have emerged, formed by the husbands of the female members of the mothers' committees. In December 2004, an opinion poll revealed that 86 per cent of the Lima population would be interested in voluntary membership of a citizens' security committee.[30] The political authorities confirm the popular acclaim for neighbourhood security: 'Wherever there are police stations there are civil security committees, *serenazgos* and district committees who assist the police. The number of committees for neighbourhood security is steadily growing, and that would be impossible if the police were considered a repressive and anti-citizen institution.'[31] Police programmes for citizens' participation are generally appreciated by the public. As part of the police reform in 2001, a directorate of 'community policing' was officially established. In April

TABLE 7.5 Trust in local authorities and local organizations (percentages)

Most trusted authorities and institutions in declining order		Membership of organizations in declining order	
Church	76	Religious organizations	39
Ombudsman	49	Neighbourhood organizations	25
Municipal authorities	46	School and family organizations	22
District authorities	43	Women's organizations	21

Source: Authors' elaboration of Tanaka and Zárate (2002: 11, 20), based on public opinion polls in 2001 and 1999.

2004 more than 55,000 *juntas vecinales de seguridad ciudadana* (neighbourhood security committees) were functioning in Peru, of which 22,500 were established in Lima (Yépez Dávalos 2004: 167). Several 'friendship with the police' programmes were initiated, of which the *policía escolar* (school police) project, with nearly 5,000 schools participating and 107,000 children involved (51,500 in Lima), is the most successful (ibid.: 169–77).

Nowhere are the police identified with brutal repression or rough action. On the contrary, municipal authorities and the local police generally enjoy a good, or at least a reasonable, reputation. The results of a recent research project on democracy and citizens' participation corroborate the picture of generalized trust in local authorities and local organizations (Table 7.5).

Conclusion

Despite the poverty, informalization and proliferation of slums in Lima Metropolitana, the city appears to have avoided the worst manifestations of urban insecurity and violence. The relative density of active grassroots and community-based organizations (which, together with the security forces, managed to keep Shining Path at arm's length during the internal conflict), progressive and sensitive local and regional administrations, supportive policies for the informal sector, and a police force with a civic orientation that has managed to avoid, by and large, practices of corruption and harassment, appear to be the main explanatory factors.

An interesting point remains the obvious fit, even interdependence, between the police and the civilian security committees. Confidence-building between local citizens' organizations and local law enforcement is apparently the key to participative policing. The comparative advantages are enormous: the lack of governance voids and of disputed urban territories, the lack of *traficantes* (local drug lords) and other illicit armed actors who take over the regulatory functions of the legitimate institutions of order and justice, the relative non-existence of large-scale criminal gangs and aggressive youth groups. In general, this is the result of a long-term policy of mitigation of harsh social exclusion, notwithstanding the overall process of poverty and informalization that Peru, even more than other Latin American countries, has endured since the mid-1970s. In spite of the huge differences in the government styles of the military in the 1970s, the two civilian governments in the 1980s and the dictatorial populism of Fujimori in the 1990s, in terms of a reduction of the severe social exclusion of the urban poor and the *informales*, all three proved relatively benevolent with respect to popular organizations.

Finally, it was the informalization process itself which initiated the emergence of three different kinds of popular organization: originally the organizations prompted by the urban land invasion, which later became the various committees of slum dwellers in the 1970s; the organizations of the self-employed and the self-financing network of interdependent micro-entrepreneurs in the 1980s and 1990s; and then the panoply of self-defence and citizens' security committees established during the last twenty years, first as a consequence of the internal armed conflict (the self-defence committees during the war and the counter-insurgency campaigns against Shining Path), then transforming themselves into the urban neighbourhood protection associations. The contradictions arising from the *desborde popular* – the disappearance of the nationwide institutions of the formal economy, society and political order and the surfacing of localized, ad hoc associations of migrants, *informales* and *vecinos* in the working-class districts – produced the social capital that favoured a minimum degree of social incorporation of the metropolitan population and prevented the creation of enclaves of violence inhabited by second-class citizens and controlled by criminal armed actors.

Notes

* We thank Rosa Vera Solano, our research assistant at the Instituto de Estudios Peruanos in Lima.

1 For an account of this internal war, see Hatun Willakuy (2004) and Degregori (2005).

2 Data provided to the authors by Fernando Villarán, minister of labour and employment, during an interview, 23 August 2002.

3 For an overview of the Fujimori years, see Degregori (2001) and Kruijt and Tello (2002).

4 Here we use data published by Kruijt et al. (2002: 20ff.).

5 'Pedro Pablo Kuzynski, Minister of Economy and Finance, confirmed yesterday [...] that the government does not have any concrete proposal to reconvert or rationalise the informality of labour. "Sure, Peru has a very high percentage of informal workers, up to 70 per cent of the national total [...] The most important theme to resolve is the formalisation of labour, the only way to ensure that the labour force can account with adequate wages and salaries, pensions and social security"' (*El Comercio*, 9 January 2005).

6 The *cono norte* accounts for 26 per cent of the population of metropolitan Lima, the *cono este* for 16 per cent and the *cono sur* for 20 per cent (Matos Mar 2004: 132–3, 149–53).

7 A phenomenon observed not only in the Andean countries but in most countries of Latin America (Alba Vega and Kruijt 1995).

8 See, for instance, the studies of Blondet (1991) and Córdova (1996).

9 Administrative subdivision of the larger *barriadas* in Lima.

10 Interview with Efrain Salas, adviser to the president of the Congress Committee of Labour, 12 January 2005.

11 For an analysis of these organizations, see Degregori et al. (1996), Starn (1999) and Fumertón (2002).

12 *Serenazgos* were originally citizens' committees with police functions in the vice-royalties of Mexico and Peru of the seventeenth and eighteenth centuries.

13 Popular corruption of 'watchman'.

14 For an analysis of these years, see González Manrique (1993).

15 Of which only 74,000 are performing police services. The police officer corps is somewhat less than 8,500. The leadership ranks are: one lieutenant general, thirty generals and 384 colonels. Of the total police force in Lima, only 24 per cent is recruited from 'old' Lima and 76 per cent from the three cones; 42 per cent comes from the northern cone alone (Perfíl del policía peruano 2004: 57, 55, 22).

16 *El Comercio*, 28 December 2004.

17 Ibid., 22 June 2003.

18 Interview with Efrain Salas.

19 Statistics quoted by Yépez Dávalos (2004: 39).

20 Vice-minister and later minister Gino Costa describes his first day at the office: 'Fernando [Rospigliosi] and I were the only civilians there present, with my parents, my daughters and some family members. Also present was Carlos Basombrío, who a couple of weeks later would join our team of three. The salon was full to bursting with officers in uniform, generals and colonels of the police. During the 1990s the ministry was completely militarised during the years of [minister] Briones and afterwards, from 1997 on, politicized with the people of [minister] Dianderas, Hurtado Esquerre and Ketín Vidal' (Basombrío Iglesias et al. 2004b: 183).

21 Interview with Fernando Rospigliosi, twice minister of internal affairs and once in charge of national intelligence between 2001 and 2004, and Carlos Basombrío, vice-minister in charge of the national police between 2001 and 2004, 13 January 2005.

22 Ibid.

23 Ibid.

24 A reliable statistic: insurance companies always verify a robbery claim.

25 Interview with Wilfredo Pedreza, director general of the INPE (National Penitentiary Institute), Ministry of Justice, 12 January 2005.

26 Director General Pedreza (interview, 12 January 2005) remarks: 'In the Lurigancho penal complex, 60 per cent of the actual inmates were previously detained in a juvenile correction centre. The average detention time of the convicts is two years. There is a kind of internal self-government, with proper codes of conduct and a proper system of sanctions and punishment. That way the Lurigancho is a sort of university of delinquency. The state, unintentionally, supplies all the ingredients for a subsequent criminal career.'

27 In Lima, in 1999, twenty-four deaths and thirty-seven woundings were attributed to youth gang violence (Yépez Dávalos 2004: 69).

28 Between January and October 2004, 695 cases were reported in Lima and nearly 2,000 in Peru (*La República*, 4 November 2004).

29 Then again, 64 per cent of Lima's population approve of popular lynching (Associated Press, Mexico, 11 November 2004).

30 Associated Press, Mexico, 12 December 2004.

31 Interview with Fernando Rospigliosi and Carlos Basombrío Iglesias, 13 January 2005.

8 | Living in fear: how the urban poor perceive violence, fear and insecurity

CATHY McILWAINE AND CAROLINE O. N. MOSER

While the increasingly ubiquitous violence permeating Latin American cities affects all sectors of society, it is the urban poor who experience it most acutely. Little is known, however, about how the poor themselves actually perceive violence and its associated fear and insecurity. Indeed, most research has tended to focus either on elite perceptions or on external academic interpretations of their experiences. As a result, there is widespread ignorance of how the poor really live with violence on a daily basis. Furthermore, when the views of the poor *are* recognized, there is a tendency to homogenize them. This homogeneity generally rests on perceptions of them either as experiencing urban violence disproportionately and uniformly, or as being inherently dangerous (Caldeira 2000, on Brazil). The latter view in particular has bolstered the emergence of widespread fear and insecurity in Latin America, which has been perpetuated by sensationalizing by the media (Arriagada and Godoy 2000).

In an effort to counter this widespread stereotyping of the urban poor, the current chapter will focus on their perceptions of violence at the community level rather than those of the elite, researchers or the media. While reflecting themes that are pertinent to the whole of urban Latin America, and acknowledging that there are huge variations between countries as well as within them (Hojman 2004), the chapter will draw on empirical material from urban Colombia and Guatemala. This is based on a study of eighteen low-income urban communities carried out in 1999 using a participatory urban appraisal (PUA) methodology. This, we argue, is one of the most effective ways of exploring how the poor themselves perceive urban violence, fear and insecurity because it allows them to voice their opinions from a host of identity standpoints in terms of gender, age, ethnicity and so on.[1,2]

In challenging simplistic conceptualizations of experiences of violence among the urban poor, this chapter focuses on a series of core issues around which the discussion is structured. The first is to stress the huge diversity and complexity of violence among the poor as both victims and perpetrators. The second is to highlight how fear of violence is not experienced solely by the middle and upper classes as is often assumed; the poor also experience widespread insecurity which undermines the nature of social relations in low-income neighbourhoods. This has important spatial implications for the poor both in terms of how they conduct their daily lives and in their physical marginalization in purportedly violent communities. Again, this challenges existing research, which tends to focus exclusively on how the elite manage and manipulate public space in cities. The third issue revolves around the legitimization of violence among the urban poor in terms of how a wide range of perverse organizations emerge in contexts of extremely high levels of violence. It is often regarded as legitimate either to join an organization involved in the perpetration of violence as a reaction against widespread exclusion and marginalization, or to condone violence as defence in terms of extra-judicial organizations providing protection. This then relates to how inadequate public security and state protection of the urban poor act as a major justification for legitimizing violence. On a more positive note, the final short section highlights the non-violent and gendered nature of coping with violence, emphasizing the role of women's groups and childcare provision in generating trust at the local level.

The diversity and complexity of violence among the urban poor

It is now well established that violence in Latin American cities is becoming ever more widespread (Cruz 1999; Koonings and Kruijt 1999). While all sectors of society are affected by such burgeoning violence, the poor tend to experience it disproportionately compared with the middle and upper classes. Although the wealthier population are increasingly having to deal with property-related violent crime, such as vehicle theft and kidnapping (Briceño León and Zubillaga 2002), the severity of violence experienced by the urban poor is usually much greater. Beyond some in-depth ethnographic accounts of violence in low-income communities (Auyero 2000, on Argentina), statistical analyses based on homicide figures that show concentrations in poor areas (Barata et al. 1998, on Brazil), or media reports that consistently misrepresent the incidence of violence everywhere (Dammert and Malone 2003, on Chile), however, little is known about the actual nature of violence among the poor in cities. It is this ignorance which has led to the stereotyping of the urban poor as harbingers of violence, and their communities as hotbeds of conflict.

When the poor are actually consulted in a broadly systematic way, it emerges that not only is violence increasingly dominating their lives, but it is becoming ever more diverse and complex. In drawing on our own research in eighteen urban poor settlements in Colombia and Guatemala violence emerged as an overwhelming preoccupation. When people were asked which problems affected their lives, violence represented almost half of all concerns in the Guatemalan communities (47 per cent) and just over 40 per cent in the Colombian settlements. Focusing on violence, people identified an astonishing array of different types. In the nine Guatemalan communities, an average of forty-one different types were discussed, while in Colombia there was an average of twenty-five. In one community in Huehuetenango, Guatemala, an alarming seventy types were identified. These ranged from violence linked with the political situation in both countries, such as the guerrilla and para-military conflict in Colombia, to street-level violence including armed robbery, delinquency and muggings, to gender-based violence in the home.

In categorizing violence for policy purposes into three types (motivated either by political, economic or social power; Moser and McIlwaine 2004), it also emerged that the urban poor in both countries were least preoccupied by political violence. Instead, various types of economic violence were seen as most important in Colombia, especially that linked with drugs and robbery (accounting for 54 per cent of all types mentioned), while in Guatemala social violence was the most common concern, especially sexual attack in public places (accounting for 50 per cent of types). In the case of Colombia, this contrasts with the views of the country's *violentólogos* (violence experts), who concentrate either on the importance of political violence or on the quantitative economic consequences of crime (e.g. Rubio 1995).

While it is important to stress that people prioritized everyday economic and social violence over political violence, in reality they also viewed different types of violence as interrelated and overlapping, often in causal ways (see also Guerrero Barón 2001; Meertens 2001; Pécaut 1999, on Colombia). Widespread intra-family violence, for instance, was often cited as precipitating a host of other forms of violence, especially among young people. Violence within the home was frequently identified as a primary reason for young men joining local gangs, and as part of this getting involved in drug-related crime, robbery and a range of other types of delinquent acts. In one community in Bogotá, Colombia, a woman noted that: 'For young people who are mistreated in the home, they go into the street and do the same thing there as part of a *pandilla* [gang].' Similarly, a teacher from Guatemala City reported that: 'Those who actually join *maras* [gangs] are more likely to be young boys who have suffered at home, and have been badly treated by their fathers' (see also below).[3]

The recognition among the urban poor of causal interrelations also extended to structural factors. Although much analysis of urban violence tends to focus on structural causes linked with poverty, inequality, globalization and so on (see Winton 2004), the poor themselves are also fully aware of how their marginalized and disadvantaged position in society underlies and exacerbates urban violence. Not only was poverty repeatedly identified as a major cause of urban violence, but many people in both countries spoke of their exclusion from what they viewed as mainstream society. For instance, a group of seven teachers from Medellín, Colombia, reported how poverty led to the emergence of gangs and robbery, which in the first place was the fault of the predominant economic model that meant policies 'favour the rich and take subsidies from the poor' (see also below).

Urban poor constructions of fear: social fragmentation and spatial restrictions

As urban violence becomes increasingly endemic, so too do the fear and insecurity that it generates. While fear is firmly rooted in many Latin American societies as a result of the state-sponsored political violence of the 1970s and 1980s, and linked with torture, repression and 'disappearances' (Garretón 1992), this legacy has been compounded by the recent increase in everyday urban violence (Pearce 1998, on El Salvador). Even more complex than before, contemporary fear has thus created widespread insecurity and vulnerability as a result of the intersections of political as well as social and economic violence (Arriagada and Godoy 2000). As Rotker (2002: 9) notes: 'The city [in Latin America] has been transformed into a space of vulnerability and danger.' Also important is that the extent of fear is not necessarily directly linked with actual victimization rates among a given population. This is shown by Dammert and Malone (2003) in the case of Chile, which is regarded as one of the safest countries in Latin America, yet has high levels of fear of crime. Also, while it is acknowledged that everyone experiences fear in cities, the media have tended to demonize the poorer sectors of society and to sensationalize the crimes and violent acts perpetrated against the rich (López Regonesi 2000, also on Chile). This is especially the case with the gangs or 'maras' of Central America, which have been widely used as scapegoats in explaining increasing levels of urban violence in supposedly post-conflict societies (Moser and Winton 2002).

Also, although the rich are often assumed to live in most fear given their association with overt symbols of material consumption and their closeting behind the walls of gated communities (Vanderschueren 1996; see below), the urban poor are actually more likely to experience it in light of the extremely high levels of violence affecting their communities. This was borne out in the research communities in Colombia and Guatemala, where widespread fear and insecurity were a fact of daily life. In many settlements, people talked about violence, insecurity, fear and danger broadly interchangeably. In Colombia, people focused on insecurity (*inseguridad*) as the main term to describe everyday violence in their *barrios*, while in Guatemala people conceptualized such violence as danger (*peligro*). In Cali, Colombia, for example, a focus group of three men and three women aged between twenty-four and forty identified a range of different types of violence and insecurity that affected people in their community on different levels. This ranged from physical and verbal aggression at the individual level, which produced personal fear, to guerrilla confrontations with community members, and army accusations about people being involved with guerrilla groups leading to people feeling insecure about neighbours they didn't know. In Guatemala, another group of three young men noted how gangs represented danger at the group and city levels, and in turn were linked with drug addicts who could abuse and kill people.

Fear and social fragmentation Few community members were in any doubt that the fear and insecurity created by everyday violence had had extremely deleterious effects on the social relations of communities.[4]

Echoing findings elsewhere in Latin America (Rodgers 2003; Rotker 2002), social fragmentation was identified as a major concern in the Colombian and Guatemalan communities (see Jimeno 2001, on Colombia; ODHAG 1999, on Guatemala). Repeatedly, people complained about the 'lack of social fabric' (*falta de tejido social*) and 'lack of union' (*falta de unión*) in their neighbourhoods. Without exception, this was linked in some way with urban violence. A telling example of a causal flow diagram from three young men from Bucaramanga, Colombia (see Figure 8.1), shows how violence rooted in the family generated insecurity that was also linked with gangs, drugs, robbery, killing and delinquency. The effects of these multiple and intersecting types of violence were 'social mistrust', 'lack of unity' and 'fear', as well as the 'lack of social institutions'.

While various types of economic and social violence were consistently identified as generating mistrust, communities that had been affected by political conflict both past and present tended to have the most severely eroded social fabric. In Guatemala, the armed conflict that officially ended in 1996 had left a lasting legacy of social fragmentation, especially in communities with a predominantly indigenous population (ODHAG 1999). In one such community in Santa Cruz del Quiché, a Mayan man complained of people's difficulty in trusting each other, remembering how during the

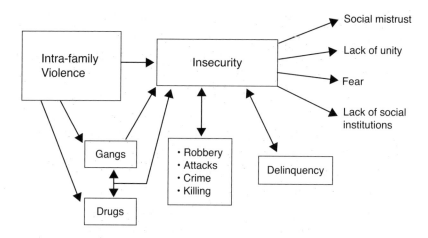

Figure 8.1 Causal flow diagram of intra-family violence in Bucaramanga, Colombia, drawn by three young men from a youth centre

conflict the army routinely killed anyone involved in a gathering of more than two people, meaning that they couldn't even hold a funeral. Mayan women were also particularly fearful of sexual violence because rape had been used as a military tool during the conflict (Moser and Clark 2001). A group of four indigenous women who had fled from Quiché to Santa Lucía Cotzumalguapa during the conflict recalled how they had to leave because of the rapes and massacres: 'We were afraid because the army came into our homes and killed the people even though they were innocent [...] many girls and women were raped by the army itself.' They went on to say that this created a deep sense of shame among the community, as well as widespread distrust which continues to the present day, not least because rape remains a major problem associated with certain organized violence groups such as the *maras.* In Colombia, communities with an active presence of guerrillas and paramilitaries had also been torn apart by fear and insecurity. In one community in Aguazul, Casanare, between 1996 and 1999, fourteen community members had been murdered by paramilitaries, two people had disappeared and ten families had fled in response to death threats. In the view of a group of four adults, this had meant that people could no longer speak to each other, generating endemic mistrust, a lack of solidarity and widespread individualism.

Regardless of the types of violence that generated it, people repeatedly complained of <u>how fear had undermined communication</u> because of lack of trust. In one of the Bogotá communities, a woman bemoaned how in the past people were much more united and communicated with each other, yet today, because of the drugs and delinquency, young people just smoked marijuana, there was no collaboration and a lack of mutual respect. Similarly in San Marcos, Guatemala, a woman complained that 'no one gets involved in the lives of others' because of a lack of trust. As a result, communities were beset by multiple petty conflicts over issues such as access to water, market stalls and land tenure. In Guatemala City, for instance, a programme to distribute and legalize plots of land for housing (see Cabanas Díaz et al. 2001) created such ill feeling that one resident who challenged the community leaders received death threats and had her house set on fire with her family inside. Thus, a lack of trust tends to generate further mistrust and conflict (see Winton 2005, on Guatemala).

Fear, spatial restrictions and area stigma Another major consequence of living in fear linked with social fragmentation is that people's spatial mobility is severely impaired, a pattern noted elsewhere (see Pain 2001). While discussions of the spatial manifestations of violence in Latin America are often associated with how the elites in cities manage violence and fear (see Caldeira 2000, on Brazil; Rodgers 2004a, on Nicaragua), the urban poor also experience restrictions on their movement. Indeed, the fortification of the rich in their residential enclaves and the increasing privatization of public space have effectively encouraged the marginalization of the poor, exacerbating their experiences of insecurity (Caldeira 1999; Cárdia 2002; De Souza 2001).

In Colombia and Guatemala, extensive spatial restrictions were manifested in people routinely avoiding certain areas of communities that they associated with danger and violence. Commonly, these included areas where gangs and drug users congregated, such as parks, particular street corners, river banks or specific houses known to be frequented by those involved in violence. In Bogotá, two young men who described themselves as *'jóvenes sanos'* (healthy young men, meaning they were not drug addicts) explained how they changed their route from their college to home in order to avoid the 'hangouts' of the local drug users and pushers. Alternatively, people stayed indoors wherever possible, as a man from Medellín, Colombia, noted: 'you have to stay at home so as not to get involved with the groups of gangs on the street corners, you can't let your children out for fear that they'll be hit by stray gunfire' (see also Katzman 1997, on Uruguay). Figure 8.2 highlights explicitly how, in Guatemala City, fear influenced how a mother and daughter negotiated their lives in their *colonia*. Significantly, not only was their spatial freedom affected by fear of sexual violence in particular, but their movement after dark was severely restricted. This was repeated everywhere, with an adult woman from Girón, Colombia, pointing out in relation to drug addicts: 'people can't go out in

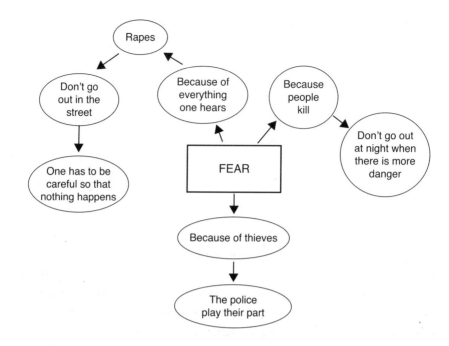

Figure 8.2 Causal flow diagram of fear in La Merced, Guatemala City, drawn by a mother (aged thirty-eight) and daughter (aged sixteen) in a tortilla-making enterprise

the evening [...] you can't send a girl or even a boy out alone because they'll get caught up with them'.

While these limitations on mobility within urban poor communities were widespread, they were coupled with segregation at the level of the city itself. Again, as found elsewhere in Latin America, the extent to which violence was experienced disproportionately in urban poor communities has meant that these neighbourhoods have become synonymous with urban conflict (Caldeira 2000). In Colombia and Guatemala, many people discussed the phenomenon of 'area stigma', which referred to the so-called bad reputation or '*mala fama*' of urban poor communities because of their extensive experience of violence. In both countries, these were often called 'red zones' (*zonas rojas*), signifying that they were dangerous. For instance, a young man from Bucaramanga, Colombia, who had graduated from high school, said that every time he applied for a job, he was automatically dismissed because he came from an urban poor settlement. His *barrio* was routinely associated with delinquency, drug consumption and robbery: 'Just because we are from Ciudad Norte no one will give us work and they think that all of us here are thieves.' Similarly, in Esquipulas, Guatemala, a group of community leaders complained how, until recently, the mayor, municipality and the town's population labelled their *colonia 'rojo'* (red), making it out of bounds for everyone except residents.

In light of these extensive spatial restrictions, together with silence or isolation being the preferred option for living, social interaction within communities was severely undermined. People were often too afraid to leave their homes except for essential visits for work and education. Involvement in community affairs was subsequently affected as most meetings took place in the evenings, and any spontaneous involvement with others was marred by suspicion (see also Cárdia 2002, on Brazil). When people did try to venture beyond their communities, they faced stigmatization by the wider city population through the stereotyping of poor neighbourhoods as being uniformly populated by the criminal and violent. In this context, it is perhaps not surprising that violence, fear and insecurity become mutually reinforcing and people in urban poor communities search out new and often equally violent ways of surviving.

The legitimization of violence among the urban poor I: the emergence of perverse social organizations

As informal social relations and solidarity within communities are ruptured by violence, the institutional landscape of urban poor communities is also fundamentally affected. One of the main characteristics of this changing landscape throughout Latin America has been the emergence of organized violence groups that provide a perverse mechanism for coping with conflict and many of the causes that underlie it.[5] Furthermore, they effectively act to legitimize violence in certain contexts; there is often widespread tolerance and support for extra-judicial violence in areas where the rule of law on the part of the state does not reach (see also Sanjuán 2002, on Venezuela; Zaluar 2000, on Brazil).[6]

Significant attention has been paid to the emergence of a violent gang culture that has been permeating cities. Found in Brazil, Colombia, Ecuador, El Salvador, Guatemala, Mexico, Honduras, Peru and Venezuela, these gangs are often blamed for a host of different types of violence (ERIC/IDESO/IDIES/IUDOP 2004; Rodgers 2003). Although they are overwhelmingly associated with urban poor neighbourhoods, their activities are felt by urban dwellers far beyond their confines. This has been fuelled by widespread media attention that exaggerates violent gang activities, especially in terms of how they affect the middle and upper classes (Moser et al. 2005). Other organized criminal gangs are also thought to be proliferating throughout the region, especially those linked with drugs trafficking found extensively in Brazilian cities (Zaluar 2001), but also in cities such as Managua, Nicaragua (Rodgers 2003). In some countries, gangs linked with drugs trafficking and other types of organized crime have merged with politically motivated guerrilla and paramilitary groups, as in Colombia (see, for example, Gutiérrez Sanín and Jaramillo 2004, on Medellín), or are formed by those demobilized after civil conflict, as in Guatemala (PNUD 1998).

From the perspective of the urban poor themselves, living in a poor neighbourhood is often synonymous with negotiating a range of organized violence groups. In the Colombian research communities, organized violence groups were both numerous and hugely diverse. In one community in Cali, Colombia, for instance, thirty-seven armed groups were identified by local residents (see, for example, Figure 8.3 on their perceived prevalence by community leaders). As in other Colombian communities, these ranged from gangs of friends who 'hung out' and engaged in various types of crime and violence (known as *parches*, *combos* or *galladas*), to groups of delinquents involved in organized crime (*oficinas* or *bandas*), and those more politically motivated and sophisticated groups, such as the various militias, guerrillas and paramilitaries, together with social cleansing groups (see also Riaño-Alcalá 1991). Many of these groups overlapped, while others operated in isolation or fought among themselves. In Medellín, a nineteen-year-old gang member who belonged to the Los Muchachos gang recalled how in the past the *comuna* had been run by a militia comprising reinserted ex-guerrilla members (from the M-19) who never consulted with the community and monopolized extortion activities. He and his friends formed Los Muchachos in order to chase the militias out. Yet following the disappearance of the militias a wide range of *combos* emerged, some comprising former militia members. This fluidity of different violent actors was coupled with a multiplicity of different types of violence, being variously political, economic and social in nature (see also Gutiérrez Sanín and Jaramillo 2004).

In Guatemala, organized violence groups were less diverse but were heavily dominated by the youth gangs or *maras*. Although groups of thieves and delinquents were also found, *maras* were the most common and provoked most consternation in communities. With specific names such as the MS (Mara Salvatrucha), the M18 or La 18 (both of which derived from Latino gangs in Los Angeles), or White Fence, Rockers, Calambres, Escorpiones and Los Duendes, they were also distinct from other groups because of their cultivation of a group identity, reflected in a 'uniform' of baggy jeans, as well as their involvement in social violence.[7] This included revenge fighting among

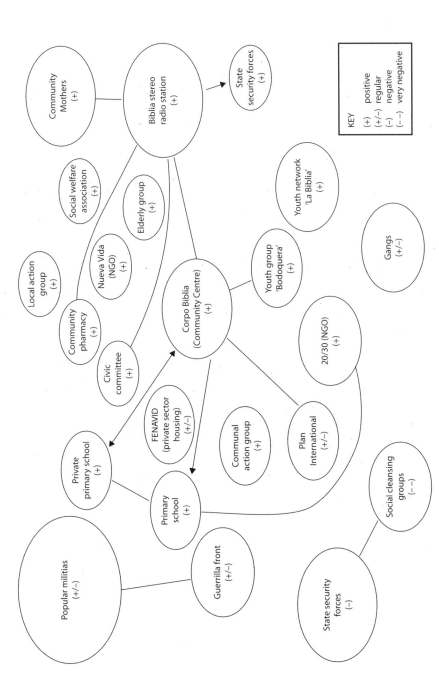

Figure 8.3 Institutional mapping of El Arca, Cali, Colombia, prepared by four community leaders

themselves over women, alcohol or music, but primarily intra-gang warfare over ownership, control and defence of 'turf'. *Maras* were also repeatedly held responsible for rape as a young woman from Santa Lucía Cotzumalguapa noted: 'the *maras* grab young girls and rape them [...] the girls are then left pregnant and single mothers'.[8]

While outside low-income urban neighbourhoods these local violence brokers are viewed as homogeneous and universally harmful, among the urban poor themselves a much more ambiguous relationship with them is evident, both as members of these groups (a minority) and as those who live with them on a daily basis (the majority). Both membership and support for these groups can therefore legitimize violence in the face of few alternative options.

Membership of perverse organizations: challenging exclusion and fear In terms of why people become involved in organized violence groups, joining a gang or other perverse social organizations is often the most logical thing to do in order to cope with the exigencies of life and a pervasive sense of marginalization and exclusion (see also Cruz 2004). In Girón, Colombia, for example, a group of six young men noted how 'we're not recognized or taken into account', which meant they got involved in drugs, vagrancy and delinquency. As noted earlier, joining a gang was often an escape from intra-family violence, abuse or parental neglect, especially for young men. As a young woman from Chinautla, Guatemala, noted: 'children grow up without love so they stay in the streets and look for love from the *maras*; what their families don't give them, the *maras* do' (see also Smutt and Miranda 1998, on El Salvador).

Also extremely significant was that membership of organized violence groups provided a livelihood and a valid career option depending on the type of group; neighbourhood gangs such as the *maras*, *pandillas* and *combos* provided mainly casual earnings, while the guerrilla and paramilitary organizations offered a regular income and career prospects, with the low-level drug traffickers somewhere in between (see also Suárez 2000). In Medellín, Colombia, five young men, all members of a *combo,* recounted how they had first joined a *parche* and participated in some petty theft of watches, shoes and bicycles, both as a hobby and to support themselves. They then formed a *combo* and, after the murder of many of their co-members, began robbing goods vehicles and cars in order to fund their war with the militias. In some Colombian communities particularly affected by conflict, families also implicitly condoned membership of organized violence groups to ensure that their own livelihood needs were met. For instance, in Aguazul, an adult woman noted that mothers encouraged their sons to join different types of organizations in order to maximize their income – one the guerrillas, one the paramilitaries and one a criminal gang.

Robbery and violent attacks are also an issue of power and a way of people asserting themselves in the face of societal inequalities. For instance, the same *combo* members from Medellín, whose idol was Che Guevara, felt that stealing from the rich was justified as they were poor. Similarly, a forty-year-old Mayan woman from Santa Lucía Cotzumalguapa, Guatemala, commented that the *maras* 'kill those who have money' (see Vanderschueren 1996). Membership of an organized violence group also provided personal protection from the widespread violence around them (Winton 2005). This was especially important in communities where there was a lot of inter-gang warfare and where the state was unable or unwilling to provide efficient public security measures.

While various types of exclusion invariably prompted initial membership of organized violence groups, somewhat ironically this membership often further exacerbated marginalization and danger. A member of the Los Muchachos in Medellín, Colombia, said that he felt alienated by the community because people ran away when he passed their houses because they were afraid. Even more serious was the fact that membership itself was often synonymous with death, with many members of organized violence groups getting killed through intra- and inter-gang warfare or crackdowns against them by state security forces or extra-legal groups, such as those involved in social cleansing. A young man in Cali pointed out in relation to the *combos*, 'So many young people have been murdered, few get out alive.' This situation prevails throughout Latin America, with murder being a common cause of death among young men in particular in many countries (Restrepo 1997, on Colombia). Murder is further exacerbated everywhere because of the high circulation levels of firearms (Muggah 2001).

Thus, while exclusion is the primary engine behind the formation of these perverse organizations, insidious fear is central to their functioning, reinforced by the use of violence. This was especially evident in the communities in Colombia where small-scale drug dealing was commonplace. Highly hierarchical and violent perverse networks emerged to control the sale and distribution of drugs. In one community in Bogotá, for example, a thirty-four-year-old woman whose two children were involved in drug distribution described the authoritarian and gendered network that operated in her community. Most streets had two male '*cabezas*' (heads) who provided the drugs and controlled their sale, but were not residents. They distributed drugs through male or female distributors called '*jibaros*'. The *jibaros* controlled one or two '*taquilleros*', who actually sold drugs, using murder as their way of enforcing their power. *Taquilleros* themselves rarely killed, but would still use force against those customers who didn't pay up on time.

Perverse organizations as protection and defence Although perverse organizations are generally viewed as negative forces by communities, there is often substantial ambiguity in people's attitudes towards them. This reflects the perceived protective role that many violence brokers play in community life (Zaluar 2001, on Brazil). In the face of few alternatives, dire necessity leads community residents to encourage or at least passively condone the presence of violent groups.

In an assessment of trust in social institutions in the research communities in Colombia across all nine communities, almost one-fifth of people felt that perverse organizations had a positive function because of their vigilance roles. This was especially marked in Medellín, Colombia, where the community was dominated by the Los Muchachos gang, which had been established primarily to protect the *barrio* from other militias (see earlier). As one resident reported: 'Los Muchachos look after the *barrio* and they collaborate with people.'

Importantly, people were also able to differentiate between perverse organizations that work for the common good of the community and those that work for their own benefit. In Guatemala, for instance, the *maras* were fairly universally reviled and feared, yet social cleansing and lynching groups were frequently praised for their extra-judicial killings. Reflecting wider public opinion in the country (see Ferrigno 1998), in one *colonia* in Guatemala City, a group of eight young women stated that lynching in their community was effective in dealing with robbery and rape (see also Goldstein 2003, on Bolivia).

Attitudes towards such groups and people are fragile, however. In Esquipulas, Guatemala, an ex-army officer called Tito had taken it upon himself to eradicate all the community's 'undesirables' and delinquents. While initially welcomed, his reign of terror over the *colonia* began to get out of hand as he evolved into a paid assassin and was eventually killed by other vigilantes. Similarly, in Cali, Colombia, people recognized the 'good *capuchos*' (hooded gunmen) who looked after the community, while the 'bad *capuchos*' robbed them. One adult woman noted that: 'The good hoods have large guns and protect the community,' while 'the bad hoods have small guns, are badly dressed and they're the ones that rob'.

The legitimization of violence among the urban poor II: inadequate state security and judicial protection

As suggested above, underlying the tolerance and legitimization of perverse organizations throughout Latin America, as well as their proliferation, is widespread mistrust of the state security forces and the state (Call 2000; Cuadra 2003). While this mistrust permeates all segments of society, the urban poor are especially affected, with their communities often becoming 'no-go' areas for the security forces, or becoming targets for heavy-handed police tactics. In the Colombian communities, this was reflected in the fact that the police, army and judicial system were the second-most mistrusted set of organizations after those involved explicitly and illegally in the perpetration of violence. A similar pattern prevailed in Guatemala, where almost two-thirds of people didn't trust the army and the police.

In both countries, the police were singled out as the main source of mistrust because of their non-delivery of security for citizens in urban poor areas. In Bucaramanga, Colombia, a young man pointed out that: 'the police cause more problems than they solve', while another in Medellín noted that they were so mistrusted that people didn't collaborate with them: 'If I see someone getting killed here and the police arrive and ask questions, I say nothing. Here it's better that way.' In most Colombian communities people complained that they were afraid of the police because they were widely involved in the perpetration of violence. In Bucaramanga, a group of young men reported how the police would enter their *barrio* firing their guns in order to frighten people. They then harassed people by constantly asking for papers and bribes. Indeed, in one extreme example from a community in Bogotá, local residents noted how the police ran a well-organized system of extortion from drug dealers: eight-man police patrols worked three shifts a day, with each officer receiving 2,680 pesos (US$1.70) per shift. Drug dealers and users usually complied with the police's demands because of fear of being killed either by them directly or by the social cleansing groups that were reportedly run by the police.

In Guatemala, the situation was more complex as the country was undergoing widespread reform of the police at the time of the research and so people made a distinction between the so-called 'former' force – the National Police (Policía Nacional, PN) and the reformed police force – the National Civil Police (Policía Nacional Civil, PNC).[9] The PN was universally condemned as corrupt, violent and ineffective. In a community in Guatemala City, a young man reported: 'after 1995, violence increased because of the aggression of the police [...] the police hit us without a motive'. The reformed PNC were

131

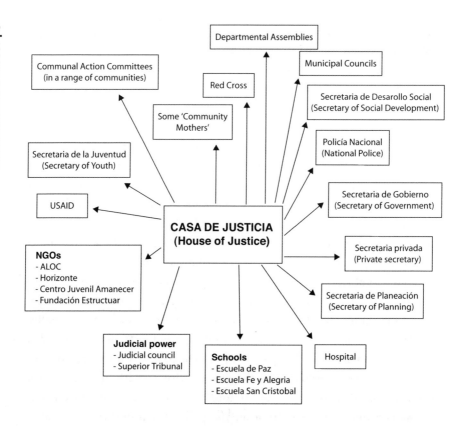

Figure 8.4 Diagram of institutional linkages of the Casa de Justicia (House of Justice) in Bucaramanga drawn by the director and two employees

generally welcomed, and people in some communities were hopeful about change. One woman in Esquipulas, for instance, pointed out that they had intervened in domestic disputes, something that the 'old police' would never have done, while another commented that overall: 'we feel more protected now than before'. Mistrust remained, however, especially among the indigenous population, because of the police's role in the counter-insurgency campaign (Kruijt 1999). In Santa Cruz del Quiché, a focus group of young indigenous people maintained that 'the police are really bad because they are not helping the community and they are interested only in causing damage because they don't practise justice' (see Glebbeek 2001 for further details on Guatemala; also Call 2003, on police reform in El Salvador).

Such mistrust of the police related to a wider perception of impunity and a lack of faith in the judicial system which pervade the entire region. Although Colombia has historically had a much more established judicial system than Guatemala, the general perception among the urban poor was

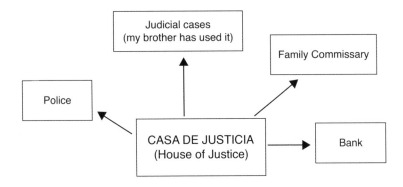

Figure 8.5 Diagram of the function of the Casa de Justicia (House of Justice), Bucaramanga, drawn by a mother of two children

that the state's legitimacy was declining. This was linked with repeated claims that there was no such thing as justice in urban poor communities. Instead, Colombian communities functioned by virtue of what was called variously the 'law of the strongest', the 'law of knives' or 'the law of defence', with perverse organizations taking justice into their own hands. In Guatemala, even the mayor of Esquipulas identified lack of justice as one of the main concerns affecting the town, caused by the 'lack of application of justice by the judges', 'lack of police agents' and 'fear of police agents'. The outcome had been massacres and fights, especially revenge killings and people taking the law into their own hands.

While the urban poor tended to direct their mistrust of the state at the police force, they also had little confidence in any other components of the judicial system. This was illustrated most poignantly by perceptions of a community-based justice initiative, the Casa de Justicia (House of Justice), in Bucaramanga. This was designed to improve access to conciliation and legal services for low-income people, and was located within the *barrio* itself.[10] Perceptions as to its efficacy and utility, however, varied greatly between those running it and the potential users, highlighting the huge gulf between the state and the urban poor in terms of trust. Drawn by the director of the Casa de Justicia and two of his employees, Figure 8.4 shows their perceptions of the programme's function in terms of its institutional links, suggesting a high level of integration of the programme with local organizations. In contrast, Figure 8.5, drawn by a local resident, associated it with only four roles. This sentiment was repeated by a group of young men, one of whom noted: 'No one trusts the Casa de Justicia [...] It is the same as the police; it plays the same role.'

Living in fear

Although the middle and upper classes can deal with the ineffectiveness of public security systems by using privatized security services, the urban poor are invariably left with no other option but to informalize protection of their communities through the various types of perverse social organizations discussed above (see also Kincaid 2000). Thus, the flourishing of these groups becomes both a cause and an effect of heightened levels of violence. Ultimately, it increases the insecurity felt within urban poor communities, exacerbating fear and, in turn, encouraging even further incidences of violence.

Non-violent coping: a gendered response

While the use of force to cope with everyday violence, whether legitimate or illegitimate, is often a common reaction throughout the cities of Latin America, the urban poor also develop non-violent mechanisms. In particular, in the Colombian and Guatemalan communities, people recognized the importance of rebuilding social relations as a way of curbing and preventing everyday violence in the first place. Indeed, in terms of all the types of solutions identified by community members, around half in both countries cited building social relations or social cohesion as an effective solution. This related more specifically to issues such as generating more dialogue and trust at the community level, as one woman from Guatemala City noted: 'we need to communicate well and advise each other and we have to treat our children well to create trust in the community'. Actively establishing new community organizations was also considered important, as another woman, also from Guatemala City, stated: 'we have to organize ourselves and raise awareness in the community in order to reduce violence'.

As discussed above, however, the role of social organizations in communities was very ambiguous. Not only were many organizations or groups involved in the perpetration of violence, many were actively mistrusted by the community at large. Yet some groups were more trusted than others, in particular organizations run by or associated with women. Among membership organizations in Colombia, for instance, women's organizations and childcare groups, both run by women, were the most trusted of all groups (by 88 per cent). In Guatemala, while there were far fewer such organizations, where they did exist they were generally highly trusted (by 76 per cent). Of particular significance in both countries was the role of the childcare providers, and especially of the state-supported 'Community Homes' (*Hogares Comunitarios*) in Colombia. These are managed and run entirely by local women who, as 'Community Mothers' (*Madres Comunitarias*), provide childcare from their homes with a small subsidy from the government. Each community had around eight to nine Community Homes operating according to horizontal management patterns and often forming a network of organizations and people in the community trusted not just by other women but by young and old of both genders. Such was their integral role in the community that some people (a group of young men from Bucaramanga) suggested that community violence reduction projects should be run through Community Homes.

While in Guatemala specific women's organizations were less widespread and integrated into the social fabric of communities compared with Community Homes in Colombia, they were still very important in some communities. In one community in Guatemala City, for example, there were six organizations, outnumbered only by churches and neighbourhood committees, which generally were held in very high esteem by everyone. For many, the largest of these, UPAVIM (Unidas para Vivir Mejor – United to Live Better), provided women with their only lifeline in terms of childcare and income-generating activities, as well as forming the main locus for organizing in the community. In addition, individual women were more likely to be perceived as institutions in their own right than were men. For example, in one of the Guatemala City communities, everyone turned to Doña Elsa when they had a problem, either personal or with their neighbours, as she was widely trusted and thought to be impartial in conflict resolution.

Therefore, while it is important not to fall into the trap of essentializing women as peacemakers and men as warmongers (see, for example, Moser and Clark 2001), evidence from Colombia and Guatemala pointed to the gendered nature of trust at the community level. More specifically, women and the organizations run and managed by them were more likely to invoke trust than others associated with men. Also, they were often felt to be more successful in building sustainable social relations that, in turn, were thought to help to prevent the incidence and spread of everyday violence.

Conclusions

This chapter has highlighted the importance of exploring how the urban poor perceive and experience violence. Although their views are often silenced or ignored, it is this section of the population in Latin America which experiences urban violence, fear and insecurity most acutely on a daily basis. In focusing on the experiences of the urban poor in Colombia and Guatemala, the chapter has shown not only how widespread this violence has become, but also how insidious it is in terms of eroding the social fabric of these communities, and undermining people's spatial mobility. Ultimately, this has served to generate yet more exclusion and more violence. In a context of extensive fear and social fragmentation, violence also becomes legitimized through the emergence of a host of diverse perverse organizations. On the one hand, and from the perspective of those who have joined these groups, these provide a forum for the urban poor, and especially the young, to challenge the multiple forms of exclusion they experience. On the other hand, and from the point of view of the wider community members, these groups often provide the only form of protection available within stigmatized and marginalized areas. The existence of these groups is invariably necessary because of an almost complete lack of trust in the role of the state, and especially the police, in providing public security. Coupled with widespread impunity, often the only option for the urban poor is to take the law into their own hands.

While the future may appear to be bleak for the urban poor both in the research communities and in Latin America as a whole, it is also important to note that they are also highly resilient in the face of extreme circumstances. This resilience is all the more notable when compared with the panicked reactions of the middle and upper classes, who can remove themselves so much more easily from violent situations and retreat into their walled enclaves. Repeatedly, examples emerged from our research of people defying the violence and fear that dominated their lives and fighting for a better future for their communities. People, and women in particular, were trying to rebuild the social relations within their communities through local organizations, such as women's groups and childcare facilities. Thus, the urban poor, despite being marginalized in terms of the protection they receive from the state, and in terms of their voices being heard by policy-makers and researchers, are still managing to cope with the conflict and violence that pervade their existence as residents of poor *barrios* in Latin American cities. Unfortunately, however, sometimes this coping itself takes on a violent face.

Notes

1 The study was conducted by the authors together with eight teams of forty local researchers. In Colombia, a total of 1,414 people participated in focus group discussions, with 1,860 taking part in Guatemala. This research was part of the 'Urban Peace Program', directed by Caroline Moser when Lead Specialist for Social Development in the Environmentally and Socially Sustainable Development Department of the Latin America and Caribbean Region of the World Bank. It was funded by the Swedish International Development Authority (Sida). In Colombia, research was conducted in three communities in Bogotá, and one respectively in Cali, Medellín, Bucaramanga, Girón, Yopal and Aguazul. In Guatemala, research was undertaken in four communities in Guatemala City, and one respectively in Huehuetenango, San Marcos, Esquipulas, Santa Cruz del Quiché and Santa Lucía Cotzumalguapa (see Moser and McIlwaine 1999, 2004).

2 The empirical work on which this chapter is based has been discussed in much greater detail in Moser and McIlwaine (2004).

3 It is also important to point out that as well as being interrelated, different types of violence are often manifested in multiple ways. For instance, political violence can take on an economic guise when the guerrilla groups impose their various illegal taxes and levies (known as '*vacunas*' or vaccinations), or economic violence can become inherently political (see also Gutiérrez Sanín and Jaramillo 2004).

4 Elsewhere we have discussed the effect of violence on social relations using the concept of social capital (see, for example, McIlwaine and Moser 2001). For reasons of brevity, however, in terms of being able to explain and justify the use of the concept theoretically, we have chosen here to focus on social relations.

5 The functioning of other productive social organizations is also affected by violence. In Colombia and Guatemala, it was found that, in a context of high levels of fear and insecurity, service delivery organizations were more prevalent than those involving membership. In addition, organizations run externally and often in a hierarchical manner were more common and more likely to be trusted within communities (McIlwaine and Moser 2004).

6 We have also considered the issue of tolerance in relation to drug- and alcohol-related violence in Colombia and Guatemala (see ibid.).

7 Gang culture throughout Central America is related to the post-conflict return migration of many individuals and their families from El Salvador, Honduras and Mexico, as well as deportation from the United States.

8 *Maras* were primarily male dominated although a few female *maras* existed. Two groups were identified in Santa Cruz del Quiché, Las Chicas Big (literally the Big Girls), with more than twenty members, who were the girlfriends of members of the male gang Los Calambres, while the other, Las Chicas (the Girls), was a female gang in its own right.

9 Police reform was implemented as part of the 1996 peace accords as an element of 'The Agreement on the Strengthening of Civilian Power and the Role of the Armed Forces in a Democratic Society', through which the government agreed to form a new civilian police force (Call 2000).

10 The Casa de Justicia programme, focusing mainly on social violence, works to promote conflict resolution, to facilitate access to the judicial system in urban poor communities with high levels of violence, and to educate people on human rights issues (Moser et al. 2000).

Epilogue: Latin America's urban duality revisited

DIRK KRUIJT AND KEES KOONINGS

When in the 1980s and early 1990s the phenomenon of urban informality and the consolidation of the slum cities in Latin America became a conventional research theme among anthropologists, sociologists, human geographers and political scientists, the complex nature of the urban and metropolitan configurations was analysed in terms of poverty. In studies about big-city problems in North America and the European Union, the urban poor were typified as an emerging urban underclass, representing 10–15 per cent of the municipal population. The Latin American urban poor and *informales* form a considerably larger portion of the metropolitan population, oscillating between 35 and 65 per cent. Their situation now clearly transcends conventional notions of poverty. Reconsidering the case studies of this book, one cannot possibly ignore the conceptual rearrangements emerging from the different chapters.

In spite of the analysis of the previous period, it is not specifically the poverty and misery which widen the gap between two kinds of citizens and which produce the fractured urban cityscape. Poverty and misery did not disappear; they became a consolidated problem, to be taken into consideration by whatever kind of municipal and national government is in power. It is, however, the persistent social exclusion, even spatial segregation and territorial concentration, of a different kind of citizenship which strikes the reader as a common denominator. If urban informality was formerly associated with fragmented labour markets and cheap and exploitative employment structures, informal citizenship is to be ascribed to the second generation of the *informales*, within their territorial boundaries, their stigmatized *favelas*, *zonas rojas*, *barriadas*, *villas* or *comunas de miseria*. It is no longer the culture of poverty which prevails; it is the culture of violence, of hostility, of disintegration, of desolation, the life expectancy of being a second-class citizen. It is the living and the pursuit of livelihood in enclaves of insecurity and violence. It is the emergence of a new kind of proletarian class, belonging to their own segregated territories, not immediately revolutionary because they are intent on survival, on making a decent or maybe an indecent living, on coping with precariousness and despair, with violence and fear. It is living in governance voids, where the legitimate authorities are often absent and where their incidental presence, symbolized by police assaults, is generally hostile and aggressive.

The long-term absence of legitimate authority is a multiplier that transforms governance void into a variety of other voids: a segmented or fragmented labour market, a standard career of income instability, a disintegration of social protective networks associated with decency and human security. The absence of the legitimate institutions and representatives of law and order creates a justice void by default: new authorities take over, sometimes political adventurers or local religious leaders with orthodox gospels preaching puritanism and abstinence, sometimes emerging entrepreneurs of the a-legal or the illicit economy (the *traficantes*), sometimes criminal gang leaders and racketeers, sometimes the tattooed bosses of youth gangs and *maras*, sometimes an honest and straightforward community leader. In most cases the danger is the emerging uncivil society of violence brokers and local gangsterism, fostering other role models, another justice system, enforcing the alternative to law and order by other regulations and inconsiderate and ruthless sanctions, substituting unprincipled incivility for morality and decency. We are, of course, not describing new traits of a culture of poverty and informality, but the reality of the violence enclaves and the despondency of the informal citizens.

Does it make sense to speak of contested urban spaces? We think the thematic explorations and case studies in this book demonstrate a variety of contested spaces. In strictly territorial and human geographical terms, we have seen literal contestation over the control of space. Deserted by formal, legal institutions, the spaces of poverty and exclusion and their control are contested by uncivil or armed actors for reasons of profit and power. This cannot be done without a certain degree of alternative, parallel legitimacy. This is the legitimacy of protection and the imposition of 'law and order', lubricated by a peculiar and strenuous mix of loyalty and intimidation. The controlled space is then constantly defended against intruding rivals, be they other gangs or the security forces of the state. In this setting, peaceful grassroots actors find it hard (but not impossible) to contest social and institutional space within their communities and to organize or claim the delivery of public goods and services. Individual citizens negotiate their social space (that is, place and time) in the face of real or perceived dangers. Finally, the contestation of space acquires a symbolic edge through meaning, belonging and stigmatization. What does it mean to live in exclusion zones and under collective forms of anxiety? What does it mean to be stigmatized as the 'alien other' on the basis of living in a particular neighbourhood?

In our book we present two extreme metropolitan cases: Rio de Janeiro and Lima. Rio de Janeiro is the city where the police are considered to be the citizen's enemy in the hundreds of *favelas*. When the police make their presence known, it is by assault. When Violeta Parra sang 'about the difference' (*Yo canto a la diferencia*) she portrayed the Chilean armed forces as 'coming from another planet'. In Rio it is the well-armed, specialized police forces, attacking like a platoon of Rambos, wreaking havoc in mostly futile attempts to re-establish law and order among the desolate *favela* citizens. The customary situation is that mafia leaders extort from shopkeepers and local entrepreneurs. In contemporary Rio de Janeiro and in Mexico City the antithesis is true: when drug *traficantes* and local gang bosses refuse to pay the 'recommended' increases in regular fees, the police enforce local taxes on crime by violent intrusion into 'the other territories'. Meanwhile, in Lima, the overall poverty and precariousness in the three slum cones are mitigated by the reduction of social exclusion. A generation of prudent municipal authorities and at least one generation of local leadership within the *barriadas* have contributed to the attenuation of the consequences of massive pauperism and misery, at least partially integrating the slums into the city and the city into the slums.

In Latin America, the amalgam of (urban) exclusion, poverty and informality has also changed the political landscape. Popular volatility is actually decisive in presidential elections and oustings. In fact, the voices and the votes of the informal citizens are decisive in presidential elections. A new phenomenon is the 'democracy of the street', the popular movements that removed their governments by means of street demonstrations, hunger marches and road blockades. In Bolivia it happened twice between 2000 and 2005. Ecuador and Argentina have fared even better: three presidents have been forced out in Ecuador (one of them was declared insane), while in 2001 Argentina had to cope with five presidents in two weeks. Peruvian president Fujimori similarly had to resign in 2000 after popular marches and city centre occupations. Popular movements frustrated a coup attempt against President Chávez in Venezuela in 2002. 'Democracy of the street' is at least an alternative to the traditional military coup, so endemic from the 1950s until the 1990s. It is, all in all, a 'civilian' or 'popular' change of government without the threat of the traditional military dictatorship, which was the norm of non-electoral government adjustments in the nineteenth and twentieth centuries. Nevertheless, it is also an expression of the latent distrust of the poor, the *informales* and the excluded vis-à-vis 'formal' society and political order, and it may give rise to a new series of anti-politicians like Menem in Argentina and Fujimori in Peru at the end of the twentieth century. One can predict the advent of a new generation of neo-populist leader of a plebiscitarian authoritarianism, whose political careers will start with control of the urban popular movements followed by national aspirations in presidential elections.

To counteract the deepening cracks in Latin America's urban class structure and the breach of dual citizenship within its fractured territories, only long-term public policies of integration, explicit reduction of exclusion and trust-building can be successful. One may think of the Brazilian model of municipal participative budgeting, successfully adopted in urban post-war El Salvador. The Chilean model of municipal administration could also be used for inspiration. One may also think of active improvement in relations between citizens and the police, taking into consideration the apparently successful Peruvian model of community policing and local security committees. One could improve the planning and managing capacity of the municipal and local authorities, promote their democratic election, provide leadership and cadre training programmes for the upcoming *dirigentes* of the urban *villas*, *barriadas, favelas* and *comunas*, as well as the lower and middle management of the urban popular movements and the *juntas vecinales* at the neighbourhood level. One may think of special security arrangements organized with the collective leadership of the metropolitan areas. Ultimately, all this implies a transfer of budgetary resources and attention from the 'First World' segments to the 'Third World' segments of metropolitan society.

Research about violence perpetrators is not plentiful but it is increasing. Most authors of the chapters included here make use of the results of recent empirical research and conceptual debates. What is maybe still in its initial stages is the very necessary research on the emerging aspirations to legitimacy on the part of representatives of the illicit, rough or criminal economy, not just within the governance void and violence enclaves. Although empirical research (in terms of opinion polls, reported periodically by, for example, *Latinobarómetro*) has been undertaken on the sentiments and beliefs of the urban poor, the *informales* and the excluded, we know only a little about the structure of the generalized distrust of the excluded of the formal economy and society. The embryonic ideological expressions of the newly arising popular movements, the feelings of disaffection, hostility, estrangement and alienation of the urban desolate and the excluded, require a conceptual review. It is a crucial review in the light of the intriguing question we formulated at the end of Chapter I, here posed in a slightly different way: How stable is Latin America's democracy under the stress of an uneasy equilibrium between 'acceptable' levels of exclusion and 'acceptable' levels of violence?

About the authors

Roberto Briceño-León is Professor of Sociology at the Central University of Venezuela and Director of the Social Science Research Laboratory (LACSO) in Caracas, Venezuela. He has published widely on violence and citizenship, urban sociology, social structure, oil-exporting societies and the social dimensions of public health.

Hector Castillo Berthier is Senior Researcher at the Institute of Social Studies of the Universidad Nacional Autónoma de México. His publications include work on urban problems, such as garbage, wholesale food markets, youth, gangs, applied research, and popular culture in Mexico and Latin America.

Carlos Iván Degregori is currently Professor of Latin American Studies at Princeton University. Between 2001 and 2004 he was a member of the Truth and Reconciliation Committee in Peru and editor of its findings. His research interests include indigenous societies in the Andean region, armed conflict and post-conflict reconstruction in Peru and urban informality and exclusion in Lima.

Kees Koonings is Associate Professor of Latin American Studies at Utrecht University. His research interests include urban and regional development, citizenship and social movements, conflict and violence, the military, and democratization, particularly in Brazil and Colombia.

Dirk Kruijt is Professor of Development Studies at Utrecht University. His research interests include urban informality and exclusion, the military and democracy, and (ethnic) conflict and post-war reconstruction, especially in the Andean region and Central America.

Elizabeth Leeds is a Visiting Scholar at the Center for Latin American and Caribbean Studies at New York University. Her research interests and publications focus on issues of local-level democracy, urban violence and public safety, with a particular focus on Brazil.

Cathy McIlwaine is a Senior Lecturer in the Department of Geography, Queen Mary College, University of London. Her research focuses on issues of poverty, survival strategies, and gender and urban violence, mainly in Latin

America, although she has also worked in South-East Asia and sub-Saharan Africa. She is currently researching the livelihood strategies of Colombians living in London.

Caroline O. N. Moser is currently a Visiting Fellow at the Brookings Institution, Washington, DC, and a Senior Research Associate at the Overseas Development Institute, London. Her research interests include urban violence and insecurity and women's organizations in conflict and peace processes, particularly in Colombia; inter-generational asset building and poverty reduction strategies in Ecuador; and gender and development.

Wil Pansters is Associate Professor in the Department of Cultural Anthropology at Utrecht University. His research interests include regional and urban politics, *caciquismo*, political culture, and higher education in Latin America, particularly Mexico.

Dennis Rodgers is a Lecturer in Urban Development at the Geography and Environment Department of the London School of Economics. His research interests include violence, crime (in particular youth gangs), local responses to political and economic crisis, urban poverty, and the work practices of multilateral bureaucracies.

Ralph Rozema is a junior researcher (PhD candidate) in the Centre for Latin American and Caribbean Studies, Department of Anthropology, Utrecht University, and a news editor at Radio Netherlands. He has conducted research on the reconstruction process in rural Peru and the armed conflict and the peace process in Medellín, Colombia.

Bibliography

Abramovay, M. and M. Das G. Rua (2002) *Violência nas Escolas*, Brasília: UNESCO.

Acosta, M. and R. Briceño-León (1987) *Ciudad y Capitalismo*, Caracas: Ediciones de la Biblioteca de la Universidad Central de Venezuela.

Alba Vega, C. and D. Kruijt (1995) *La Utilidad de lo Minisculo. Estudios sobre la Informalidad y la Microempresa en México, Centroamérica y los Paises Andinos*, Mexico City: Colegio de México.

Alvarado, A. (2000) 'La seguridad pública', in G. Garza (ed.), *La Ciudad de México en el Final del Segundo Milenio*, Mexico City: Colegio de México, pp. 410–19.

— (2002) 'Violence and crime in Mexico City. An analysis of Reforma's newspaper crime surveys', Paper presented at the 6th World Conference on Injury Prevention and Control, Montreal, 12–14 May.

Alvarado, A. and D. Davis (2001) 'Cambio político, inseguridad pública y deterioro del estado de derecho en México: algunas hipótesis en torno del proceso actual', in A. Alvarado and S. Artz (eds), *El Desafío Democrático de México: Seguridad y Estado de Derecho*, Mexico City: Colegio de México, pp. 115–43.

— (2003) 'Participación democrática y gobernabilidad en la Ciudad de México: el reto del PRD en la transición política', *Estudios Sociológicos*, XXI(61): 135–66.

Alvarado, A. et al. (2005) 'Respuestas vecinales a la inseguridad pública en la Ciudad de México', Paper presented at the international conference 'Diálogo Internacional para la Reforma Policial en México', Mexico City, 22/23 February.

Alvito, M. (2001) *As Cores de Acari: Uma Favela Carioca*, Rio de Janeiro: Editora FGV.

Appadurai, A. (1996) *Modernity at Large: Cultural Dimensions of Globalization*, Minneapolis: University of Minnesota Press.

Arango Durán, A. (2003) 'Indicadores de seguridad pública en México: la construcción de un sistema de estadísticas delectivas', USMEX 2003–2004 Working Papers Series, <http://usmex.ucsd.edu/justice>.

— (2004) *Sistema de Información Delictiva. La Estadística de Seguridad Pública en México*, Mexico City/San Diego: INACIPE/Center for US–Mexican Studies.

Arriagada, I. and L. Godoy (2000) 'Prevention or repression? The false dilemma of citizen security', *CEPAL Review*, 70: 111–36.

Arroyo, M. (2003) 'Evaluando la "estrátegia Giuliani": la política de cero tolerancia en el Distrito Federal', USMEX 2003–2004 Working Papers Series, <http://usmex.ucsd.edu/justice>.

Arteaga Botello, N. (2004) *En Busca de la Legitimidad. Seguridad Pública y Populismo Punitivo en México, 1990–2000*, Alicante: University of Alicante.

Auyero, J. (2000) 'The hyper-shantytown: neo-liberal violence(s) in the Argentine slum', *Ethnography*, 1(1): 93–116.

Azaola, E. (2004) 'Imagen y autoimagen de la policía en la Ciudad de México',

Paper presented at the 'Diálogo Internacional para la Reforma Policial en México', 22/23 July.

— (2005) 'Desde Tláhuac hacia la sociedad que queremos: notas para una agenda', Unpublished paper distributed by the Instituto para la Seguridad y la Democracia AC, Mexico City.

Balbín, J. (2004) 'Politik: Eine Demobilisierung mit vielen Fragen', *Kolumbien - aktuell*, 380, <www.kolumbien-aktuell.ch/Publikationen/ka380.html>.

Baptista, A. (1997) *Teoría Económica del Capitalismo Rentístico*, Caracas: IESA.

— (2004) *El Relevo del Capitalismo Rentístico, Hacia un nuevo Balance del Poder*, Caracas: Fundación Polar.

Barata, R. B., M. C. Sampaio de Almeida Ribeiro, M. B. Lauretti da Sulva Guedes and J. Cássio de Moraes (1998) 'Intra-urban differentials in death rates from homicide in the city of São Paulo, Brazil 1988–1994', *Social Science and Medicine*, 47(1): 19–23.

Barcellos, C. (2003) *Abusado: O Dono do Morro Dona Marta*, Rio de Janeiro/São Paulo: Editora Record.

Basombrío Iglesias, C. (2004) *Seguridad Ciudadana y Actuación del Estado. Análisis de Tendencias de Opinión Pública*, Lima: Instituto de Defensa Legal.

Basombrío Iglesias, C., G. Costa Santolalla, M. Huerta Barrón and S. Villarán de la Puente (2004a) *Activistas de Derechos Humanos a cargo de la Seguridad y el Orden en el Perú*, Lima: Instituto de Defensa Legal.

Basombrío Iglesias, C., M. Boluarte, L. Caparrós, E. Castro, G. Costa, M. J. Gamarra, A. Gazzo, M. Huerta, G. Prado, F. Rospigliosi, R. Valdés, R. Vargas, D. Vera and S. Villarán (2004b) *Manejo y Gestión de la Seguridad. De la Reforma al Inmovilismo*, Lima: Instituto de Defensa Legal.

Bastos, S. (1998) 'Los indios, la nación y el nacionalismo', in C. Dary (ed.), *La Construcción de la Nación y la Representación Ciudadana en México, Guatemala, Perú, Ecuador y Bolivia*, Guatemala, pp. 87–157.

Beato, C. and R. Souza (2003) 'Controle de homicídios: a experiência de Belo Horizonte', *Segurança Cidadã e Polícia na Democracia. Cadernos Adenauer*, IV(3): 51–74.

Beato, C., K. Rabelo and A. de Oliveira (forthcoming) *Reforma Policial no Brasil*, Washington, DC: World Bank.

Blondet, C. (1991) *Las Mujeres en el Poder. Una historia de Villa El Salvador*, Lima: Instituto de Estudios Peruanos.

Blondet, C. and C. Trivelli (2004) *Cucharas en Alto. Del Asistencialismo al Desarrollo Local: Fortaleciendo la Participación de las Mujeres*, Lima: Instituto de Estudios Peruanos.

Bolívar, T. (1995) 'Urbanizadores, constructores y ciudadanos', *Revista Mexicana de Sociología*, 57(1): 71–87.

Bolívar, T. and J. Baldo (1995) *La Cuestión de los Barrios*, Caracas: Monteavila Editores.

Bolívar, T., M. Guerrero, I. Rosas, T. Ontiveros and J. de Freitas (1994) *Densificación y Vivienda en los Barrios Caraqueños. Contribución a la Determinación de Problemas y Soluciones*, Caracas: MINDUR-CONAVI.

Borsdorf, A. (2002) 'Barrios cerrados en Santiago de Chile, Quito y Lima: tendencias de la segregación socio-espacial en capitales andinas', in L. F. Cabrales Barajas (ed.), *Latinoamérica: Países Abiertos, Ciudades Cerradas*, Guadalajara: UNESCO and University of Guadalajara, pp. 581–610.

Briceño-León, R. (1986) *El Futuro de las Ciudades Venezolanas*, Caracas: Ediciones Lagoven.

— (1990) 'Contabilidad de la muerte', in *Cuando la Muerte Tomó la Calle*, Caracas: Ediciones Ateneo.

— (1991) *Los Efectos Perversos del Petróleo: Renta Petrolera y Cambio Social*, Caracas: Fondo Editorial Acta Científica Venezolana/Consorcio de Ediciones Capriles.

— (2000) 'Los hilos que tejen la vida social', in A. Baptista (ed.), *Venezuela del Siglo XX, Historias y Testimonios*, vol. 1, Caracas: Fundación Polar, pp. 125–53.

— (2002) 'La nueva violencia urbana en América Latina', in R. Briceño-León (ed.), *Violencia, Sociedad y Justicia en América Latina*, Buenos Aires: CLACSO, pp. 13–26.

— (2003) 'Para comprender la violencia', in R. Briceño-León and R. Pérez Perdomo (eds), *Morir en Caracas. Violencia y Ciudadanía*, Caracas: Law Faculty, UCV.

— (2005a) 'Dos décadas de violencia en Venezuela', in *Terrorismo, Violencia y Criminalidad*, Caracas: Ediciones Venezuela Positiva.

— (2005b) 'Petroleum and democracy in Venezuela', *Social Forces, the Journal of Social Issues*, 83: 1–32.

— (2005c) 'Urban violence and public health in Latin America: a sociological explanatory model', *Cadernos de Saude Pública*, 21(6): 1,629–64.

Briceño-León, R. and V. Zubillaga (2002) 'Violence and globalization in Latin America', *Current Sociology*, 50(1): 11–29.

Briceño-León, R., A. Camardiel and O. Ávila (2002) 'El derecho a matar en América Latina', in R. Briceño-León (ed.), *Violencia, Sociedad y Justicia en América Latina*, Buenos Aires: CLACSO, pp. 383–440.

— (2003) '¿Tiene la policía derecho a matar a los delincuentes?', in R. Briceño-León and R. Pérez Perdomo (eds), *Morir en Caracas. Violencia y Ciudadanía*, Caracas: Law Faculty, UCV.

Cabanas Díaz, A., E. Grant, P. I. del Cid Vargas and V. Sajbin Velásquez (2001) 'The role of external agencies in the development of El Mesquital in Guatemala City', *Environment and Urbanization*, 13(1): 91–100.

Caldeira, T. (1999) 'Building up the walls: the new pattern of spatial segregation in São Paulo', *International Social Science Journal*, 147: 55–66.

— (2000) *City of Walls: Crime, Segregation and Citizenship in São Paulo*, Berkeley: University of California Press.

— (2002) 'The paradox of police violence in democratic Brazil', *Ethnography*, 3(3): 235–63.

Call, C. T. (2000) 'Sustainable development in Central America: the challenges of violence, injustice and insecurity, Central America 2020', Working Paper no. 8, Hamburg: Institut für Iberoamerika-Kunde.

— (2003) 'Democratisation, war and state-building: constructing the rule of law in El Salvador', *Journal of Latin American Studies*, 35: 827–62.

Cano, I. (1997) *Letalidade da Ação Policial no Rio de Janeiro*, Rio de Janeiro: ISER.

Carbonetto, D., J. Hoyle and M. Tueros (1988) *Lima: Sector Informal*, Lima: DESCO (2 vols).

Cárdia, N. (2002) 'The impact of exposure to violence in São Paulo: accepting violence or continuing horror', in S. Rotker et al. (eds), *Citizens of Fear: Urban Violence in Latin America*, New Brunswick, NJ, and London: Rutgers University Press, pp. 152–83.

— (2004) 'Violação de direitos e violência: relações entre qualidade de vida urbana, exposição à violência e capital social', in L. C. Queiroz (ed.), *Metrópoles: Entre a Coesão e Fragmentação, a Cooperação e Conflito*, São Paulo: Editora Fundação Perseu Abramo, pp. 325–56.

Castillo Berthier, H. (2005) 'Pandillas y violencia', Unpublished paper distributed by the Instituto para la Seguridad y la Democracia AC, Mexico City.

CEPAL (2004) *Panorama Social de America Latina 2004*, Santiago: CEPAL.

Chen, C.-Y., G. Bidegain, A. Pellegrino and D. López (1986) *Aspectos Demográficos del Proceso de Urbanización: Pasado, Presente y Futuro*, Working Paper no. 25, Caracas: UCAB.

Chevigny, P. (2003) 'The populism of fear. Politics of crime in the Americas', *Punishment and Society*, 5(1): 77–96.

CONATEL (2004) *Observatorio Estadístico*, Caracas: CONATEL.

Concha-Eastman, A. (2002) 'Urban violence in Latin America and the Caribbean, dimensions, explanations, actions', in S. Rotker et al. (eds), *Citizens of Fear: Urban Violence in Latin America*, New Brunswick, NJ, and London: Rutgers University Press, pp. 37–54.

Coordinaciones Territoriales de Seguridad Pública y Procuración de Justicia. Guía de Coordinación (2001) Mexico City: Gobierno del Distrito Federal.

Córdova, P. (1996) *Liderazgo Femenino. Estrategias de Supervivencia*, Lima: Fundación Friedrich Ebert.

Costa, G. and C. Basombrío Iglesias (2003) *Liderazgo Civil en el Ministerio del Interior. Testimonio de una Experiencia de Reforma Policial y Gestión Democrática de la Seguridad en el Perú*, Lima: Instituto de Estudios Peruanos.

Cruz, J. M. (1999) 'La victimización por violencia urbana: niveles y factores asociados en ciudades de América Latina y España', *Pan American Journal of Public Health: Special Issue on Violence*, 4(5): 259–302.

— (2004) 'Pandillas y capital social en Centroamérica', in ERIC/IDESO/IDIES/IUDOP (eds), *Maras y Pandillas en Centroamérica: Pandillas y Capital Social*, vol. II, San Salvador: UCA Editores.

Cuadra, S. (2003) 'Globalization and the capacity of violence to transform social spaces: some critical points about Latin America debate', *Crime, Law and Social Change*, 39: 163–73.

Dammert, L. and M. F. T. Malone (2003) 'Fear of crime or fear of life? Public insecurities in Chile', *Bulletin of Latin American Research*, 22(1): 79–101.

Davis, M. (2004) 'Planet of slums: urban involution and the informal proletariat', *New Left Review*, 26: 5–34.

— (2006) *Planet of Slums*, London: Verso.

Daza, A. (2001) 'Entre esquinas, cambuches, cruces y callejones', in A. Daza, G. Salazar and L. González, *Experiencias de Intervención en Conflicto Urbano*, vol. II, Medellín: Alcaldía de Medellín, pp. 61–275.

Degregori, C. I. (2001) *La Década de la Antipolítica. Auge y Huida de Alberto Fujimori y Vladimiro Montesinos*, 2nd, enlarged edn, Lima: Instituto de Estudios Peruanos.

— (2005) *Que Difícil es Ser Dios. El Partido Comunista del Perú (Sendero Luminoso) y el Conflicto Armado Interno en el Perú, 1980–1999*, PhD thesis, Utrecht: Utrecht University.

Degregori, C. I., C. Blondet and N. Lynch (1986) *Conquistadores del Nuevo Mundo: De Invasores a Ciudadanos en San Martín de Porres*, Lima: Instituto de Estudios Peruanos.

Degregori, C. I., J. Coronel, P. del Pino and O. Stark (1996) *Las Rondas Campesinas y la Derrota de Sendero Luminoso*, Lima: Instituto de Estudios Peruanos.

Douglas, M. and B. Isherwood (1979) *The World of Goods: Towards an Anthropology of Consumption*, Boston, MA: Basic Books.

Dowdney, L. (2003) *Children of the Drug Trade: A Case Study of Children in Organised Armed Violence in Rio de Janeiro*, Rio de Janeiro: 7 Letras.

Drewe, P. (1986) 'Integrated upgrading of marginal areas in Managua', *Cities*, 3(4): 333–49.

Driant, J. C. (1991) *Las Barriadas de Lima. Historia e Interpretación*, Lima: IFTA and DESCO.

El Camino por Recorrer, Documentos del Proyecto Pobreza (2001) Caracas: Universidad Católica Andrés Bello, vol. II.

ERIC/IDESO/IDIES/IUDOP (eds) (2004) *Maras y Pandillas en Centroamérica: Pandillas y Capital Social*, vol. II, San Salvador: UCA Editores.

Evangelista, H. de Araujo (2003) *Rio de Janeiro. Violência, Jogo de Bicho e Narcotráfico segundo uma Interpretação*, Rio de Janeiro: Editora Revan.

Fernandes, R. C. (2004) 'Segurança para viver: propostas para uma política de redução da violência entre adolescentes e jovens', in R. Novaes and P. Vannuchi (eds), *Juventude e Sociedade: Trabalho, Educação, Cultura e Participação*, São Paulo: Editora Fundação Perseu Abramo, pp. 260–74.

Ferraro, K. F. (1995) *Fear of Crime. Interpreting Victimization Risk*, New York: State University of New York.

Ferrigno F. V. (1998) 'El estado democrático de derecho frente al conflicto social', Paper presented at 'Foro-Taller, Linchamminetos: diagnóstico y búsqueda de soluciones', Panajachel, Guatemala, May.

Fischer, K., J. Jäger and C. Parnreiter (2003) 'Transformación económica, políticas y producción de la segregación social en Chile y México', *Scripta Nova*, VII(146 [127]), <www.ub.es/geocrit/sn/sn-146(127).htm>.

Flores Galindo, A. (1994) *Buscando un Inca: Identidad y Utopía en los Andes*, 4th edn, Lima: Editorial Horizonte.

Franco, J. (2004) *Rosario Tijeras*, Bogotá: Editorial Planeta.

Fumerton, M. (2002) *From Victims to Heroes. Peasant Counter-rebellion and Civil*

War in Ayacucho, Peru, 1980–2000, Amsterdam: Rozenberg Publishers (Thela Latin America Series).

Galli, R. and D. Kucera (2003) *Informal Employment in Latin America: Movements over Business Cycles and the Effects of Worker Rights*, Geneva: ILO/International Institute for Labour Studies (DP/145/2003).

Garretón, M. A. (1992) 'Fear in military regimes: an overview', in J. E. Corradi, P. Weiss and M. A. Garretón (eds), *Fear at the Edge: State Terror and Resistance in Latin America*, Berkeley and Los Angeles: University of California Press.

Garza, G. (2000) *La Ciudad de México en el Final del Segundo Milenio*, Mexico City: Colegio de México.

Gay, R. (2005) *Lucia: Testimonies of a Brazilian Drug Dealer's Woman*, Philadelphia, PA: Temple University Press.

Glebbeek, M. L. (2001) 'Police reform and the peace process in Guatemala: the fifth promotion of the National Civilan Police', *Bulletin of Latin American Research*, 20(4): 431–53.

— (2003) *In the Crossfire of Democracy. Police Reform and Police Practice in Post-Civil War Guatemala*, Amsterdam: Rozenberg (Thela Latin America Series).

Goldstein, D. M. (2003) '"In our own hands": lynching, justice, and the law in Bolivia', *American Ethnologist*, 30(1): 22–43.

Golte, J. and N. Adams (1987) *Los Caballos de Troya de los Invadores. Estrategias Campesinas en la Conquista de la Gran Lima*, Lima: Instituto de Estudios Peruanos.

Gómez-Cespedes, A. (1999) 'The federal law enforcement agencies. An obstacle in the fight against organized crime in Mexico', *Journal of Contemporary Criminal Justice*, 15(4): 352–69.

Gonzales, J. (2001) *Redes de Informalidad en Gamarra*, Lima: Universidad Ricardo Palma – Editorial Universitaria.

González Manrique, L. E. (1993) *La Encrucijada Peruana:De Alan García a Fujimori*, 2 vols, Madrid: CEDEAL.

González Placencia, L. (2002) *Ciudades Seguras V. Percepción Ciudadana de la Inseguridad*, Mexico City: Fondo de Cultura Económica, CONACyT, UAM-Azcapotzalco.

González Placencia, L. and R. Rodríguez Luna (2001) 'Inseguridad subjetiva y experiencias con el delito: actitudes respecto a la seguridad en Ciudad de México', *Revista Catalana de Seguretat Pública*, 8: 253–84.

Guerrero Barón, J. (2001) 'Is the war ending? Premises and hypotheses with which to view the conflict in Colombia', *Latin American Perspectives*, 28(1): 12–30.

Guimarães, E. (1998) *Escola, Galeras e Narcotráfico*, Rio de Janeiro: Editora UFRJ.

Gutiérrez Sanín, F. and A. M. Jaramillo (2004) 'Crime, (counter-)insurgency and the privatization of security – the case of Medellín, Colombia', *Environment and Urbanization*, 16(2): 17–30.

Hatun Willakuy. Versión abreviada del informe final de la Comisión de la Verdad y Reconciliación, Perú (2004) Lima: Truth and Reconciliation Commission.

Hayner, N. S. (1946) 'Crimonogenic zones in Mexico City', *American Sociological Review*, 11(4): 428–38.

Hojman, D. (2004) 'Inequality, unemployment and crime in Latin American cities', *Crime, Law and Social Change*, 41: 33–51.

Hordijk, M. (2000) *Of Dreams and Deeds. The Role of Local Initiatives in Community Based Urban Environmental Management. A Case Study from Lima, Peru*, Amsterdam: Thela Publishers (Thela Latin America Series).

Huggins, M. K., M. Haritos-Faroutos and P. Zimbardo (2002) *Violence Workers*, Berkeley: University of California Press.

Human Rights Watch (2005) *Colombia, Librando a los Paramilitares de sus Responsabilidades*, <http://hrw.org/backgrounder/americas/colombia0105-sp>.

ICER (Informe de la Coyuntura Económica Regional de Antioquia) (2005) Bogotá: Banco de la República–DANE, November.

INE (2001) *Proyecciones de Población*, Caracas: Instituto Nacional de Estadística.

Informe Estadístico Noviembre (2004) Lima: Ministerio de Justicia – Instituto Nacional Penitenciario/Oficina General de Planificación – Oficina de Estadística.

IPC (Instituto Popular de Capacitación) (2003) 'Breve recuento de los actores armadas en Medellín, década del 90', *Boletín virtual 04 'Por la vida'*, <www.corporacionpp.org.co/actualidad_Boletin_VirtualVida04.htm>.

Jaramillo Arbeláez, A. M., R. de J. Ceballos Melguizo and M. I. Villa Martínez (1998) *En la Encrucijada. Conflicto y Cultura Política en el Medellín de los Noventa*, Medellín: Corporación REGIÓN.

Jiménez Ornelas, R. (2001) 'Percepciones sobre la inseguridad y la violencia en México. Análisis de encuestas y alternativas de política', in A. Alvarado and S. Artz (eds), *El Desafío Democrático de México: Seguridad y Estado de Derecho*, Mexico City: Colegio de México, 145–72.

— (2003) 'La cifra negra de la delincuencia en México: sistema de encuestas sobre victimización', in S. García Ramírez and L. A. Vargas Casillas (eds), *Proyectos Legislativos y Otros Temas Penales. Segundas jornadas sobre justicia penal* (Doctrina Jurídica series, 129), Mexico: Instituto de Investigaciones Jurídicas, pp. 167–90.

Jimeno, M. (2001) 'Violence and social life in Colombia', *Critique of Anthropology*, 21(3): 221–46.

Junior, J. (2003) *Da Favela Para o Mundo*, Rio de Janeiro: Aeroplano Editora e Consultaria.

Katzman, C. (1997) 'Marginality and social integration in Uruguay', *CEPAL Review*, 62: 93–119.

Kincaid, A. D. (2000) 'Demilitarization and security in El Salvador and Guatemala: convergences of success and crisis', *Journal of Interamerican Studies and World Affairs*, 42(4): 39–58.

Knight, M. and A. Özerdem (2004) 'Guns, camps and cash: disarmament, demobilization and reinsertion of former combatants in transitions from war to peace', *Journal of Peace Research*, 41(4): 499–516.

Koonings, K. and D. Kruijt (eds) (1999) *Societies of Fear: The Legacy of Civil War, Violence and Terror in Latin America*, London: Zed Books.

— (2002) 'Military politics and the mission of nation building', in K. Koonings and D. Kruijt (eds), *Political Armies: Military, Politics, and Nation Building in the Age of Democracy*, London: Zed Books, pp. 9–34.

— (2004) 'Armed actors, organized violence and state failure in Latin America: a survey of issues and arguments', in K. Koonings and D. Kruijt (eds), *Armed Actors: Organised Violence and State Failure in Latin America*, London: Zed Books, pp. 5–15.

Koonings, K. and J. Leestemaker (2004) 'The demise of a model? Industrialists, globalization and violence in Medellín since 1980', in D. Kruijt, P. van Lindert and O. Verkoren (eds), *State and Development, Essays in Honour of Menno Vellinga*, Amsterdam: Rozenberg Publishers, pp. 129–44.

Kruijt, D. (1994) *Revolution by Decree. Peru 1968–1975*, Amsterdam: Thela Publishers (Thela Latin America Series).

— (1999) 'Exercises in state terrorism: the counter-insurgency campaigns in Guatemala and Peru,' in K. Koonings and D. Kruijt (eds) (1999), *Societies of Fear: The Legacy of Civil War, Violence and Terror in Latin America*, London: Zed Books, pp. 33–62.

Kruijt, D. and K. Koonings (1999) 'Violence and fear in Latin America', in K. Koonings and D. Kruijt (eds), *Societies of Fear: The Legacy of Civil War, Violence and Terror in Latin America*, London: Zed Books, pp. 1–30.

— (2004) 'The military and their shadowy brothers in arms,' in K. Koonings and D. Kruijt (eds), *Armed Actors: Organised Violence and State Failure in Latin America*, London: Zed Books, pp. 16–30.

Kruijt, D. (1994) 'The informal society', in C. Alba Vega and D. Kruijt, *The Convenience of the Minuscule. Informality and Microenterprise in Latin America*, Amsterdam: Thela Thesis (Thela Latin America Series), pp. 15–28.

Kruijt, D. and M. Tello (2002) 'From military reformists to civilian dictatorship: Peruvian military politics from the 1960s to the present', in K. Koonings and D. Kruijt (eds), *Political Armies: The Military and Nation Building in the Age of Democracy*, London: Zed Books, pp. 35–63.

Kruijt, D., C. Sojo and R. Grynszpan (2002) *Informal Citizens. Poverty, Informality and Social Exclusion in Latin America*, Amsterdam: Rozenberg Publishers (Thela Latin America Series).

LACSO (1996) *Encuesta de Actitudes y Normas hacia la Violencia*, Caracas: Laboratorio de Ciencias Sociales.

— (2004) *Encuesta de Violencia y Sistema de Justicia Penal en Venezuela*, Caracas: Laboratorio de Ciencias Sociales.

Leeds, E. (1996) 'Cocaine and parallel politics in the Brazilian urban periphery: constraints on local-level democratization', *Latin American Research Review*, 31(3): 47–82.

— (2006) 'Serving states and serving citizens: halting attempts at police reform in Brazil', *Policing and Society* (in press).

Lemgruber, J., L. Musumeci and I. Cano (2003) *Quem Vigia os Vigias? Um Estudo sobre Controle Externo da Polícia no Brasil*, Rio de Janeiro: Editora Record.

López-Montiel, A. G. (2000) 'The military, political power, and police relations in Mexico City', *Latin American Perspectives*, 27(2): 70–94.

López Regonesi, E. (2000) *Reflexiones acerca de la Seguridad Ciudadana en Chile:*

Visiones y Propuestas para el Diseno de una Política, Políticas Sociales series no. 44, Santiago: ECLAC, <www.eclac.cl>.

Lozano, R. et al. (2000) 'Capital lesionada: violencia en Ciudad de México', in J. L. Londoño et al. (eds), *Asalto al Desarrollo. Violencia en América Latina*, Washington, DC: IADB.

Macaulay, F. (2002) 'Problems of police oversight in Brazil', Working paper, Oxford: Centre for Brazilian Studies/University of Oxford.

McDonald, J. H. (2005) 'The narcoeconomy and small-town, rural Mexico', *Human Organization*, 64(2): 115–25.

McIlwaine, C. and C. Moser (2001) 'Violence and social capital in urban poor communities: perspectives from Colombia and Guatemala', *Journal of International Development*, 13(7): 965–84.

— (2004) 'Drugs, alcohol and community tolerance: an urban ethnography from Colombia and Guatemala', *Environment and Urbanization*, 16(2): 49–62.

Mahler, S. J. (2002) 'Las migraciones y la problemática transnacional: tendencias recientes y perspectivas para 2020', in K. Bodemer and E. Gamarra (eds), *Centroamérica 2020. Un Nuevo Modelo de Desarrollo Regional*, Caracas: Editorial Nueva Sociedad, pp. 160–96.

Marquez, P. (1999) *The Street is My Home*, Stanford, CA: Stanford University Press.

Marx, K. (1976) *Capital: A Critique of Political Economy*, trans. B. Fowkes and with an introduction by E. Mandel, London: Penguin.

Matos Mar, J. (1984) *Desborde Popular y Crisis del Estado. El Nuevo Rostro del Perú en la Década de 1980*, Lima: IEP.

— (2004) *Desborde Popular y Crisis del Estado. Veinte Años Después*, Lima: Fondo Editorial del Congreso del Perú.

Mauro Machuca, R. (2002) *Cambio en la Pobreza en el Perú: 1991–1998. Un Análisis a Partir de los Componentes del Ingreso*, Lima: CIES/DESCO (Investigaciones Breves series), April.

Meertens, D. (2001) 'Facing destruction, rebuilding life: gender and the internally displaced in Colombia', *Latin American Perspectives*, 28(1): 132–48.

Mejía, J. (1999) 'Espacios sociales y violencia pandillera en Lima', in W. Kapsoli, J. Mejía, L. Franco, N. Ugarriza and M. Zolezzi (1999), *Modernidad y Pobreza Urbana en Lima*, Lima: Universidad Ricardo Palma – Centro de Investigación, pp. 75–125.

Melo, M. (2002) 'Gains and losses in the favelas', in D. Narayan and P. Petesch (eds), *Voices of the Poor: From Many Lands*, New York: World Bank/Oxford University Press.

Méndez, J., G. O'Donnell and P. S. Pinheiro (eds) (1999) *The (Un)rule of Law and the Underprivileged in Latin America*, Notre Dame, IN: University of Notre Dame Press.

Mesquita, P. and A. Loche (2003) 'Police–community partnership in Brazil', in H. Früling, J. Tulchin and H. Golding (eds), *Crime and Violence in Latin America*, Baltimore, MD: Johns Hopkins University Press, pp. 179–204.

Minayo, M. C. de Souza et al. (1999) *Fala, Galera: Juventude, Violência e Cidadania no Rio de Janeiro*, Rio de Janeiro: Garamond.

MINTERIOR (2004) *Archivos de Estadísticas*, Caracas: Ministry of the Interior.

Montoya, R. (2003) 'House, street, collective: revolutionary geographies and gender transformation in Nicaragua, 1979–99', *Latin American Research Review*, 38(2): 61–93.

Morrison, A., M. Buvinic and M. Shifter (2003) *Crime and Violence in Latin America: Citizen Security, Democracy and the State*, Baltimore, MD: Johns Hopkins University Press.

Moser, C. (2004) 'Urban violence and insecurity: an introductory roadmap', *Environment and Urbanization*, 16(2): 3–16.

Moser, C. and F. Clark (eds) (2001) *Victims, Perpetrators or Actors? Gender, Armed Conflict and Political Violence*, London: Zed Books.

Moser, C. and C. McIlwaine (1999) 'Participatory urban appraisal and its application for research on violence', *Environment and Urbanization*, 11(2): 203–26.

— (2004) *Encounters with Violence in Latin America: Urban Poor and Perceptions from Colombia and Guatemala*, New York/London: Routledge.

Moser, C. and A. Winton (2002) *Violence in the Central American Region: Towards an Integrated Framework for Violence Reduction*, ODI Working Paper no. 171, London: ODI.

Moser, C., A. Winton and A. Moser (2005) 'Violence, fear, and insecurity among the urban poor in Latin America', in M. Fay (ed.), *The Urban Poor in Latin America*, Washington, DC: World Bank, pp. 125–78.

Moser, C., S. Lister, C. McIlwaine, E. Shrader and A. Tornqvist (2000) *Violence in Colombia: Building Sustainable Peace and Social Capital*, Environmentally and Socially Sustainable Development Sector Management Unit Report no. 18652-CO, Washington, DC: World Bank.

Muggah, H. C. R. (2001) 'Globalisation and insecurity: the direct and indirect effects of small arms availability', *IDS Bulletin*, 32(2): 70–78.

Navarro, J. C. and R. Pérez Perdomo (1991) *Seguridad Personal: Un Asalto al Tema*, Caracas: Ediciones IESA.

Negrón, M. (2001) *Ciudad y Modernidad. El Rol del Sistema de Ciudades en la Modernización de Venezuela 1936–2000*, Caracas: Ediciones del Instituto de Urbanismo, UCV.

Neves, P. S. da Costa, C. Rique and F. Freitas (2002) *Polícia e Democracia: Desafias a Educação em Direitos Humanos*, Recife: Edições Bagaço.

Nitlapán-Envío Team (1995) 'The crisis is bordering on the intolerable', *Envío in English*, 167: 3–13.

Noche y Niebla (2003) *Comuna 13, la Otra Versión*, Bogotá: CINEP and Justicia y Paz, <www.nocheyniebla.org/com1301.htm>.

Núñez, J.-C. (1996) *De la Ciudad al Barrio: Redes y Tejidos Urbanos en Guatemala, El Salvador y Nicaragua*, Guatemala City: Universidad Rafael Landívar/PRO-FASR.

OAS (2005) *Report on the Demobilization Process in Colombia*, Washington, DC: Organization of American States/Inter-American Commission on Human Rights, <www.cidh.oas.org/countryrep/Colombia04eng/chapter1.htm>.

OCEI (2004) *Anuario Estadístico*, Caracas: Central Office of Statistics and Information.

O'Day, P. (2001) 'The Mexican army as cartel', *Journal of Criminal Justice*, 57(3): 278–95.

ODHAG (Oficina de Derechos Humanos del Arzobispado de Guatemala) (1999) *Guatemala: Never Again! Recovery of Historical Memory Project (REMHI), Official Report of the Human Rights Office, Archdiocese of Guatemala*, London: CIIR/LAB.

Pain, R. (2001) 'Gender, race, age and fear in the city', *Urban Studies*, 38(5/6): 899–913.

Pandolfi, D. and M. Grynszpan (2003) *A Favela Fala*, Rio de Janeiro: Editora FGV.

Paris, R. (2001) 'Human security: paradigm shift or hot air?', *International Security*, 26(2): 87–102.

Pearce, J. (1998) 'From civil war to "civil society": has the end of the Cold War brought peace to Central America?', *International Affairs*, 74(3): 587–615.

Pécaut, D. (1999) 'From the banality of violence to real terror: the case of Colombia', in K. Koonings and D. Kruijt (eds), *Societies of Fear: The Legacy of Civil War, Violence and Terror in Latin America*, London: Zed Books, pp. 141–67.

— (2001) *Guerra contra la Sociedad*, Bogotá: Editorial Planeta.

— (2003) *Violencia y Política. Ensayos sobre el Conflicto Colombiano*, Medellín: Editora Hombre Nuevo.

Peetz, P. (2004) 'Zentralamerikas Jugendbanden. "Maras" in Honduras, El Salvador und Guatemala', *Brennpunkt Lateinamerika. Politk-Wirtschaft-Gesellschaft*, 5: 49–63.

Peña, G. de la (1980) *Herederos de Promesas. Agricultura, Política y Ritual en los Altos de Morelos*, Mexico City: Ediciones de la Casa Chata.

Pérez Perdomo, P. (2002) 'Contar los cuerpos, lamer las heridas: la tarea de cuantificar la violencia delictiva', in R. Briceño-León and R. Pérez Perdomo (eds), *Morir en Caracas. Violencia y Ciudadanía*, Caracas: Law Faculty, UCV.

Pérez Sáinz, J. P. (2004) 'La pobreza urbana en América central: evidencias e interrogantes de la década de los 90', in S. H. Davis, E. Gacitúa and C. Sojo (eds), *Desafíos del Desarrollo Social en Centroamérica*, San José/Washington, DC: FALCSO/World Bank, pp. 63–103.

Perfíl de la Policía Peruano (2004) Lima: Instituto de Defensa Legal.

Perlman, J. (1976) *The Myth of Marginality. Urban Poverty and Politics in Rio de Janeiro*, Berkeley and Los Angeles: University of California Press.

— (2005) *The Myth of Marginality Revisited. The Case of Favelas in Rio de Janeiro 1969–2003*, Unpublished ms.

Piccato, P. (2001) *City of Suspects. Crime in Mexico City, 1900–1931*, Durham, NC: Duke University Press.

— (2003) 'A historical perspective on crime in twentieth-century Mexico City', USMEX 2003–2004 Working Papers Series, <http://usmex.ucsd.edu/justice>.

Pinheiro, P. S. (1996) 'Democracy without citizenship', *NACLA Report on the Americas*, 30(2): 17–23.

PNUD (1998) *Guatemala: Los Contrastes del Desarrollo Humano*, Guatemala: PNUD.

— (2003) *El conflicto, callejón con salida. Informe Nacional de Desarrollo Humano Colombia – 2003*, Bogotá : PNUD/UNDP.

Portes, A. (1985) 'Latin American class structures: their composition and change during the last decades', *Latin American Research Review*, 20(3): 7–39.

— (1989) 'Latin American urbanization during the years of the crisis', *Latin American Research Review*, 24(3): 7–43.

Portes, A. and K. Hoffman (2003) 'Latin American class structures: their composition and change during the neoliberal era', *Latin American Research Review*, 38(1): 41–82.

Programa Paz y Reconciliación. Regreso a la legalidad (2005) Medellín: Alcaldía de Medellín.

Proyectos Legislativos y Otros Temas Penales. Segundas jornadas sobre justicia penal (2001) Mexico City: Instituto de Investigaciones Jurídicas.

Ramos, S. and L. Musumeci (2005) *Elemento Suspeito: Abordagem Policial e Discriminação na Cidade do Rio de Janiero*, Rio de Janeiro: Editora Civilização Brasileira.

Reames, B. (2003) 'Police forces in Mexico: a profile', USMEX 2003–2004 Working Papers Series, <http://usmex.ucsd.edu/justice>.

Renner, M. (1997) 'Small arms, big impact: the next challenge of disarmament', *Worldwatch Paper 137*, Washington, DC: Worldwatch Institute, October.

Restrepo, L. A. (2004) 'Violence and fear in Colombia: fragmentation of space, contraction of time and forms of evasion', in K. Koonings and D. Kruijt (eds), *Armed Actors: Organised Violence and State Failure in Latin America*, London: Zed Books, pp. 172–85.

Restrepo, O. L. (1997) 'Situación de la violencia juvenil en Cali', in Proceedings of the PAHO Adolescent and Youth Gang Violence Prevention Workshop, San Salvador, 7–9 May, Washington, DC: PAHO.

Riaño-Alcalá, P. (1991) '*Las galladas*: street youth and cultural identity in the barrios of Bogotá', in H. P. Diaz, J. W. A. Rummens and P. D. M. Taylor (eds), *Forging Identities and Patterns of Development in Latin America and the Caribbean*, Toronto: Canadian Scholars' Press Inc.

Ribeiro, L. C. de Q. (2002) 'Segregação, acumulação urbana e poder: classes e desigualdades na metrópole do Rio de Janeiro', *Cadernos IPPUR/UFRJ*, 16(1): 79–103.

Ribeiro, L. C. de Q. and L. C. do Lago (eds) (2004) *Metrópoles: Entre a Coesão e a Fragmentação, a Cooperação e o Conflito*, São Paulo: Editora Fundação Perseu Abramo.

Riofrío, G. (1990) *Producir la Ciudad (Popular) de los 90: Entre el Estado y el Mercado*, Lima: DESCO.

Ríos Espinosa, C. (2003) *La Política del Gobierno del Distrito Federal en Material de Seguridad y Protección a los Derechos Humanos*, Mexico City: Instituto para la Seguridad y la Democracia AC.

Robinson, W. I. (1998), '(Mal)development in Central America: globalization and social change', *Development and Change*, 29(3): 467–97.

Rocha, J. L. (2002) 'Microsalarios y megasalarios: megadesigualdad y microdesarrollo', *Envío*, 240: 17–27.

Rodgers, D. (1999) 'Youth gangs and violence in Latin America and the Caribbean: a literature survey', Latin America and the Caribbean Region Sustainable Development Working Paper 4 (Urban Peace Program Series), Washington, DC: World Bank.

— (2000) *Living in the Shadow of Death: Violence, Pandillas, and Social Disintegration in Contemporary Urban Nicaragua*, Unpublished PhD dissertation, Department of Social Anthropology, University of Cambridge.

— (2003) 'Youth gangs in Colombia and Nicaragua: new forms of violence, new theoretical directions?', in A. Rudqvist (ed.), *Breeding Inequality – Reaping Violence, Exploring Linkages and Causality in Colombia and Beyond*, Stockholm: Uppsala University (Outlook on Development Series, Collegium for Development Studies), pp. 111–41, <www.kus.uu.se/poverty&violence/PovertyViolence.pdf>.

— (2004a) '"Disembedding" the city: crime, insecurity and spatial organization in Managua, Nicaragua', *Environment and Urbanization*, 16(2): 113–23.

— (2004b) 'La globalización de un barrio "desde abajo": emigrantes, remesas, taxis, y drogas', *Envío*, 264: 23–30.

— (2006) 'Living in the shadow of death: gangs, violence, and social order in urban Nicaragua, 1996–2002', *Journal of Latin American Studies*, 38(2) (forthcoming).

— (forthcoming), 'When vigilantes turn bad: gangs, violence, and social change in urban Nicaragua', in D. Pratten and A. Sen (eds), *Global Vigilantes: Anthropology, Violence, and Community in the Contemporary World*, London: C. Hurst & Co.

Rodríguez, R. (2003) *Violência e Narcotráfico no Rio de Janeiro: Perspectivas e Impasses no Combate ao Crime Organizado*, Rio de Janeiro: Universidade Federal de Juiz de Fora, <www.defesa.ufjf.br/arq/RV>.

Rolnik, R. (1999) 'Exclusão territorial e violência', *São Paulo Perspective*, 13(4): 100–111, <www.scielo.br>.

Rothstein, F. A. (2005) 'Challenging consumption theory: production and consumption in central Mexico', *Critique of Anthropology*, 25(3): 279–306.

Rotker, S. (2002) 'Cities written by violence: an introduction', in S. Rotker with K. Goldman and J. Balán (eds), *Citizens of Fear: Urban Violence in Latin America*, New Brunswick, NJ, and London: Rutgers University Press, pp. 7–24.

Rotker, S. with K. Goldman and J. Balán (eds), *Citizens of Fear: Urban Violence in Latin America*, New Brunswick, NJ, and London: Rutgers University Press.

Rubio, M. (1995) 'Crimen y crecimiento en Colombia', *Coyuntura Económica*, XXV(1): 101–27.

Sabatini, F. and F. Arenas (2000) 'Entre el estado y el mercado: resonancias geográficas y sustentabilidad social en Santiago de Chile', *EURE*, 26(79): 95–113.

Saín, M. F. (2002) *Seguridad, Democracia y Reforma del Sistema Policial en la Argentina*, Buenos Aires: Fondo de Cultura Económica.

Salazar, A. (1993a) *No Nacimos pa' Semilla. La Cultura de las Bandas Juveniles de Medellín*, 7th edn, Bogotá: CINEP.

— (1993b) *Mujeres de Fuego*, Medellín: Corporación REGIÓN.

— (1994) 'Young assassins of the drug trade', *NACLA Report on the Americas*, May/June.

Salcedo, R. and A. Torres (2004) 'Gated communities in Santiago: wall or frontier?', *International Journal of Urban and Regional Research*, 28(1): 27–44.

Sanjuán, A. M. (1997) 'La criminalidad en Caracas: percepciones y realidades', *Revista Venezolana de Economía y Ciencias Sociales*, 3(2/3): 215–54.

— (2002) 'Democracy, citizenship and violence in Venezuela', in S. Rotker with K. Goldman and J. Balán (eds), *Citizens of Fear: Urban Violence in Latin America*, New Brunswick, NJ, and London: Rutgers University Press, pp. 87–101.

Savenije, W. and K. Andrade-Eekhoff (2003) *Conviviendo en la Orilla. Violencia y Exclusión Social en el Area Metropolitana de San Salvador*, San Salvador: FLACSO.

Savenije, W. and C. van der Borgh (2004) 'Youth gangs, social exclusion and the transformation of violence in El Salvador', in K. Koonings and D. Kruijt (eds), *Armed Actors: Organised Violence and State Failure in Latin America*, London: Zed Books, pp. 155–71.

Shelley, L. (2001) 'Corruption and organized crime in Mexico in the post-PRI transition', *Journal of Contemporary Criminal Justice*, 17: 213–31.

Silva, C. (2004) 'Abuso policial en la Ciudad de México', in M. G. Barrón Cruz et al., *Guardia Nacional y Policía Preventiva: Dos Problemas de Seguridad en México*, Mexico City: Instituto Nacional de Ciencias Penales, pp. 135–55.

Silva, H. O. de and J. de Souza e Silva (2005) *Análise da Violência contra Criança e o Adolescente segundo o Ciclo de Vida no Brasil*, Brasília: UNICEF.

Smutt, M. and J. L. E. Miranda (1998) *El Fenómeno de la Pandillas en El Salvador*, San Salvador: UNICEF/FLACSO.

Snodgrass Godoy, A. (2004) 'When "justice" is criminal: lynchings in contemporary Latin America', *Theory and Society*, 33: 621–51.

Soares, G. and D. Borges (2004) 'A cor da morte', *Ciência Hoje*, 35(209): 27–31.

Soares, L. E. (1996) 'O inominável, nosso medo', in *Violencia e Política no Rio de Janeiro*, Rio de Janeiro: ISER-Relume Dumará.

— (2000) *Meu casaco de general. 500 dias no front da segurança pública do Rio de Janeiro*, São Paulo: Companhia das Letras.

— (2004) 'Juventude e violência no Brasil contemporâneo', in R. Novaes and P. Vannuchi (eds), *Juventude e Sociedade: Trabalho, Educação, Cultura e Participação*, São Paulo: Editora Fundação Perseu Abramo.

Soares, L. E., M. V. Bill and C. Athayde (2005) *Cabeça de Porco*, Rio de Janeiro: Editora Objetiva.

Soberón, G. et al. (2003) 'La violencia como un problema de salud pública', in *Caleidoscopio de la Salud*, Mexico City: Fundación Mexicana de la Salud.

Solares, J. (1992) 'Guatemala: etnicidad y democracia en tierra arrasada', in G. Aguilera et al., *Los Problemas de la Democracia*, Guatemala: FLACSO, pp. 47–72.

Soto, H. de (1986) *El Otro Sendero: La Revolución Informal*, Lima, Instituto Libertad y Democracia.

Souza, M. L. de (1996) 'As drogas e a "questão urbana" no Brasil: a dinâmica sócio-espacial nas cidades brasileiras sob influência do tráfico de tóxicos', in I. E. de Castro et al. (eds), *Brasil: questões atuais de reorganização do território*, Rio de Janeiro: Bertrand Brasil.

— (2001) 'Metropolitan deconcentration, socio-political fragmentation and extended suburbanisation: Brazilian urbanisation in the 1980s and 1990s', *Geoforum*, 32(4): 437–48.

Souza e Silva, J. and A. Urani (2002) *Crianças no Narcotráfico: Um Diagnóstico Rápido*, Brasília: Ministério do Trabalho e Emprego/ILO-Brasil.

Starn, O. (1999) *Nightwatch. The Politics of Protest in the Andes*, Durham, NC and London: Duke University Press.

Stepan, A. (1978) *The State and Society. Peru in Comparative Perspective*, Princeton, NJ: Princeton University Press.

Suárez, A. R. (2000) 'Parasites and predators: guerrillas and the insurrection economy of Colombia', *Journal of International Affairs*, 53(2): 577–601.

Svampa, M. (2001) *Los que Ganaron: La Vida en los countries y Barrios Privados*, Buenos Aires: Editorial Biblos.

Tanaka, M. (2001) *Participación Popular en Políticas Sociales*, Lima: Instituto de Estudios Peruanos.

Tanaka, M. and P. Zárate (2002) *Valores Democráticos y Participación Ciudadana en el Perú, 1998–2001*, Lima: Instituto de Estudios Peruanos.

Taylor, C. (2002) 'Modern social imaginaries', *Public Culture*, 14(1): 91–124.

Thoumi, F. E. (2002) *El Imperio de la Droga. Narcotráfico, Economía y Sociedad en Los Andes*, Bogotá: Editorial Planeta.

Ugalde, L. (1990) *La Violencia en Venezuela*, Caracas: Monteavila Universidad Católica Andres Bello.

UNDP (1994) *Human Development Report 1994*, New York/Oxford: Oxford University Press for the United Nations Development Programme.

— (1998) *Guatemala: Los Contrastes del Desarrollo Humano*, Guatemala City: United Nations Development Programme.

— (2003) *El Conflicto, Callejón con Salida*, Bogotá: United Nations Development Programme.

Ungar, M. (2004) 'La mano dura: current dilemmas in Latin American police reform', Paper presented at the Conference on Security and Democracy in the Americas, New School University, New York, April.

Vance, I. (1985) 'More than bricks and mortar: women's participation in self-help housing in Managua, Nicaragua', in C. Moser and L. Peake (eds), *Women, Human Settlements and Housing*, London: Tavistock, 139–65.

Vanderschueren, F. (1996) 'From violence to justice and security in cities', *Environment and Urbanization*, 8(1): 93–112.

Van Reenen, P. (2004) 'Policing extensions in Latin America', in K. Koonings and D. Kruijt (eds), *Armed Actors: Organised Violence and State Failure in Latin America*, London: Zed Books, pp. 33–51.

Van Young, E. (1981) *Hacienda and Market in Eighteenth-century Mexico. The Rural Economy of the Guadalajara Region, 1675–1820*, Berkeley: University Press of California.

Veblen, T. (1902) *The Theory of the Leisure Class: An Economic Study of Institutions*, New York: Macmillan.

Vélez Rendón, J. C. (2001) 'Conflicto y guerra: la lucha por el orden en Medellín', *Estudios Políticos*, 18, January–June.

Ventura, Z. (2002) *Cidade Partida*, Rio de Janeiro: Editora Companhía das Letras (1st edn 1994).

Villa Martínez, M. I., L. A. Sánchez Medina and A. M. Jaramillo Abeláez (2003) *Rostros del Miedo, una Investigación sobre los Miedos Sociales Urbanos*, Medellín: Corporación REGIÓN.

Walton, J. (1976) 'Guadalajara: creating the divided city', in W. Cornelius and R. U. Kemper (eds), *Metropolitan Problems and Governmental Responses in Latin America*, Beverly Hills, CA: Sage.

— (1977) *Elites and Economic Development. Comparative Studies in the Political Economy of Latin American Cities*, Austin: University of Texas Press.

Ward, P. et al. (2004) 'From the marginality of the 1960s to the "new poverty" of today', *Latin American Research Review*, 39(1): 183–203.

Webb, R. and G. Fernández Baca (2001) *Anuario Estadístico. Perú en Números 2001*, Lima: Instituto Cuánto.

Willer, H. (2005) 'Las PYME del cono norte', *Ideele. Revista del Instituto de Defensa Legal*, 170: 70–75.

Winton, A. (2004) 'Urban violence: a guide to the literature', *Environment and Urbanization*, 16(2): 165–84.

— (2005) 'Youth, gangs and violence: analysing the social and spatial mobility of young people in Guatemala City', *Children's Geographies*, 3(2): 167–84.

World Bank (2000) *World Development Report 2000/2001: 'Attacking Poverty'*, New York: Oxford University Press for the World Bank.

Yépez Dávalos, E. (2004) *Seguridad Ciudadana: 14 Lecciones Fundamentales*, Lima: Instituto de Defensa Legal.

Ypey, A. (2000) *Producing against Poverty. Female and Male Micro-entrepreneurs in Lima, Peru*, Amsterdam: Amsterdam University Press.

Zaluar. A. (1994) *Condomínio do Diabo*, Rio de Janeiro: Editora da UFRJ.

— (2000) 'Perverse integration: drug trafficking and youth in the favelas of Rio de Janeiro', *Journal of International Affairs*, 53(2): 654–71.

— (2001) 'Violence in Rio de Janeiro: styles of leisure, drug use, and trafficking', *International Social Science Journal*, 3: 369–79.

— (2004) 'Urban violence and drug warfare in Brazil', in K. Koonings and D. Kruijt (eds), *Armed Actors: Organized Violence and State Failure in Latin America*, London: Zed Books, pp. 139–54.

Zubillaga, V. and R. Briceño-León (2001) 'Exclusión, masculinidad y respeto: algunas claves para entender la violencia entre adolescentes en barrios', *Nueva Sociedad*, 173: 34–78.

Zubillaga, V. and A. Cisneros (2001) 'El temor en Caracas: relatos en barrios y urbanizaciones', *Revista Mexicana de Sociología*, 63(1): 161–76.

Media articles

El Colombiano (2004) 'Cifras dicen que Medellín es más segura', 14 October, Medellín.

— (2005) 'Desmovilizados llegaron a las JAC', 23 May, Medellín.

El Mundo Magazine (2003) 'Escobar sigue vivo en Colombia ... y en su finca', 7 December, Madrid.

El Tiempo (2003) 'Así se vive en el vecindario de la Comuna 13', 6 September, Bogotá.

New York Times (2003) '800 in Colombia lay down arms, kindling peace hopes', 26 November, New York.

Semana (2004) 'Rosario, cámara, acción', 23 February, Bogotá.

— (2005) 'Medellín, El Pacificador', 25 April, Bogotá.

Washington Post (2002) 'Urban anti-rebel raid a new turn in Colombian war', 24 October, Washington, DC.

Index

- only Managua chap. mentions Davis — also most theoret

- Racial components - Brazil, Colombia; Gender components - rape in Guatemala
  Imp of [organism] in these barrios — not anarchy (drug trade Man. barrio; paras in Medellin etc)

- Generalised distrust of pop/poor/inform re. polit/judicial/form soc - not much known, but book points to urgency of finding more.
- drug trade - esp cocaine

Reasons/problem - chaps highlight several factors
connectn betn econ downturn + rise of crime /insecurity
poverty + informality + social exclusion (racial, spatial, + class)
failure of police methods + probity
state failure/ unwillingness to take respons. for learning best policy, formulating policy/practice for inclusion (soc, econ. polit)

- Public percpn of w class n'hoods - reluctn to employ; more likely to stop/search young men; heavy handed police actions eg Colom, Guat.

data on Mexico bf